MAXIMISE YOUR TRAINING SESSIONS

Football Practices for Ever-Changing Numbers and Spaces

Rob McKay

BENNION KEARNY

Published in 2023 by Bennion Kearny Limited.

Copyright © Bennion Kearny Limited

Rob McKay has asserted his right under the Copyright Designs and Patents Act 1988 to be identified as the author of this work

ISBN: 978-1-915855-15-2

All Rights Reserved. No part of this publication may be reproduced, stored in a retrieval system, or transmitted in any form or by any means, electronic, mechanical, photocopying, recording or otherwise, without the prior permission of the publisher.

This book is sold subject to the condition that it shall not, by way of trade or otherwise, be lent, re-sold, hired out or otherwise circulated without the publisher's prior consent in any form of binding or cover other than that in which it is published and without a similar condition including this condition being imposed on the subsequent purchaser.

Bennion Kearny has endeavoured to provide trademark information about all the companies and products mentioned in this book by the appropriate use of capitals. However, Dark River cannot guarantee the accuracy of this information.

Bennion Kearny Limited
6 Woodside, Churnet View Road, Oakamoor, ST10 3AE

In association with

Duktig Brand was founded by Tiffany Weimer and Adelaide Gay, two professional soccer players at the time, who wanted a soccer-specific notebook for their own personal use. While playing overseas in Sweden, the two began the process of designing and purchasing the perfect soccer notebook. With lots of advice from others and trial and error, they settled on the Trainer as the first-ever product from Duktig Brand.

Since then, Duktig Brand has sold more than 100,000 notebooks in places like the US, Canada, Sweden, Denmark, Germany, Netherlands, France, Spain, Russia, Indonesia, Australia, New Zealand, South Africa and more! There is a Duktig Brand product in each of the 50 states in the US. The company's goal is to continue to create products that are affordable and accessible while using the highest quality materials they can possibly find.

Rob McKay is a proud ambassador for Duktig Brand. To receive a 10% discount off your Duktig Brand order, use MCKAY22 at the checkout.

To my dad

Table of Contents

Chapter 1. Introduction 1

Chapter 2. Training Principles 5

Chapter 3. Playing Principles 11

Chapter 4. The Build Up Phase 21

Chapter 5. Defending In The Attacking Third 29

Chapter 6. Build-Up Third – Practices 37

Chapter 7. Middle Third In Possession 49

Chapter 8. Out of Possession – Middle Third 57

Chapter 9. Middle Third Practices 65

Chapter 10. In Possession – Final Third 79

Chapter 11. Out of Possession – Defensive Third 87

Chapter 12. Final Third Practices 95

Chapter 13. General Practices 109

Chapter 14. Conclusion 123

1. Introduction

"I'm sorry I won't make training;
the lung transplant I was observing overran" *

Training Night(mares)

You've got your numbers for training. You've formulated the perfect session. You've spent hours planning and visualising success in your mind. You even arrive early in the hope that the previous session has finished early to allow you a few extra moments to set up! No one is on the pitch before you. Result. This is going to be your best session yet.

Then it happens.

The ping of your phone.

A message.

"Won't be at training tonight because [insert your own reason] … so sorry!"

If you're lucky, that will be the only message you receive. If you're unlucky, there will be multiple messages. If you're really unlucky, you don't get any messages at all and spend the next 15 minutes keeping one eye on every car that pulls up in the anxious wait for *anyone* to show up.

Panic sets in as your perfect session suddenly isn't so perfect anymore. Suddenly, you're wracking your brain for a Plan B with levels of critical thinking a NASA scientist would envy. Cones come up; cones go down. The theme changes. It changes again. People are arriving. The warmup begins. You crawl through the darkest recesses of your brain for a session you saw that one time but can't quite remember. The warmup is over. Everyone is looking at you, ready and waiting...

We've all been there. I suspect that if you're reading this book, then you've also been there. We've all been on our way to training in the driving rain, and endless traffic, as player after player has dropped out for one reason or another. Some legitimate, some less so. From personal experience (see the top of the chapter), "Sorry, the lung transplant I was observing went long…" has yet to be beaten.

Unfortunately, this is a reality for grassroots coaches around the world. Real life often gets in the way of our ambitions. Each week, we are expected to plan and deliver a session that Pep Guardiola himself would applaud, but we are often left to salvage our sessions on little or no notice. Worse, we feel like it's only happening to us and no one else. The good news is, I can assure you that it's not just you!

"I won't be at training, my dogs just given birth; I didn't even know she was pregnant" *

The Struggle is Real

When I first began coaching, scenarios like this were a regular occurrence. Each week, I'd be in the car on my way to training or already there, hurriedly trying to adjust my session for last-minute dropouts. Anything from the weather to the traffic to whoever was at home in the Champions League could decimate my numbers by up to half. I just wasn't equipped to deal with it, and not only did I let it affect my session, I'd also take it personally.

The *English FA Level 1* course has a crucial module that introduces new coaches to the STEP principle, which guides them on how to design their sessions. However, one key point missing was for new coaches to consider how these principles might be adjusted on the fly.

The STEP Principle

Space – The space you have in which to train.

Time – The time you have in which to train.

Equipment – The equipment you have at your disposal.

People – The players and coaches that you have available.

I, like many coaches, consumed as much information as I could. I spent hours online scouring eBay, Amazon, or YouTube to find that one book or practice that I hoped would take me to the next level as a coach.

However, I'd also be very guilty (albeit despite admirable attempts to prove that I wasn't the worst coach in human history) of lifting something off the page without due consideration as to how it might be best adjusted for the players that I coached.

I would read so many coaching plans and be overwhelmed by the complexity of the conditions or put off by the volume of equipment required. Session designs that required an exact number of players were an immediate no-go, as was anything that would take an age to set up. It rains in Manchester. A lot! Often, I would find a practice I liked but then encounter unrealistic progressions or require too many players to be stood around static. It's cold, too!

Practices requiring two-thirds of a pitch or two full-size goals were off the table as I had access to neither. As was anything that needed to be set up multiple times over; the last thing I needed was bored players waiting for me to put down every cone I had at my disposal. Oh, and don't get me started on practices that include mannequins!

What I failed to understand was that it wasn't the coaching materials *but the coach reading them*. I should have been using these incredible resources for inspiration to create the best sessions for my own players rather than simply copying someone else's. I needed to develop my own ideas, principles, and beliefs. If you're reading this, then you may have had similar experiences at some point on your coaching journey.

"I fell asleep" *

I Was So Naïve

Throughout this book, I will go into detail about both my training principles and playing principles. I will demonstrate how I use these principles to build effective training sessions that consider the STEP principles, and which can also be quickly adjusted to suit the coach's needs.

The reality for many grassroots coaches is that you must plan for any number of factors whilst delivering something meaningful, challenging and enjoyable. You may only have your players for an hour a week, and you're keen to maximise your session for their enjoyment. As coaches, we all want to have the best training possible and provide the best environment for our players.

"Sorry, I forgot training was on. I was shaving my legs." *

Challenge Your Thinking

Whether you're picking up your first-ever coaching book, or picking up your 50th, my aim is to challenge you to consider your practice design to help deliver more effective and challenging sessions that maximise the resources at your disposal.

In this book, I have included practices that take into account some of the considerations that grassroots coaches might need to consider on an average training night. If we follow the STEP principles, I've attempted to design practices that can be set up whether you have a full pitch, half pitch, or even a quarter of one.

Additionally, I've deliberately left the times off each practice. You – as a coach – will know your players and how long your players should practice for. You may be a coach with 60 minutes to get everything in, or you might even have two hours.

More importantly, I've tried to consider the setup time to ensure that however long you have, you're able to hit the optimal ball rolling time for your players.

Likewise, when it comes to equipment, I've looked to work with a minimal amount. Ideally, as a minimum, we've all got balls, bibs, and cones, but where I've used goals or mini goals, I've considered how they can be substituted for cone goals.

Finally, when it comes to people, I hope that (within reason) the practices can be executed despite last-minute adjustments of numbers. For clarity, I've included even numbers in practices. If you have an odd number of players, you should be able to use a neutral player without greatly harming the realism or the repetition of the practice.

Also, I've included goalkeepers as standard. If you do not have a goalkeeper available, then consider two-touch finishes for your players to present them with a challenge in front of goal; or swap out the goal for a smaller target.

At this point, I will say that I am not suggesting – for one moment – that every practice within these pages is the best one for you and your players. What I do hope is that this book provides you with a foundation upon which you can reflect, consider, build and adapt your own principles.

Thank you for taking the time to pick up this book. I wish you the very best of luck on your coaching journey!

Rob McKay

Head Coach, University of Manchester

Actual text messages I received from players moments before training began.

2. Training Principles

"Coaching is not about controlling the outcomes.
It is about offering the learning."

Pablo Aimar

Once I had an idea of how I wanted my teams to play, I had to figure out how I wanted training to reflect that. As a coach, I felt it crucial that training supported our principles of play on match day, with sessions that reinforced this.

In all honesty, I didn't start out thinking this way. When I first got into coaching, I mimicked a lot of what I found because I saw successful coaches doing it and assumed it was the reason for their success. I had little original thinking of my own and took very little notice of their coaching points (or lack of).

I thought sessions were something to be 'done', and if players showed glimpses of it during matches, then I'd succeeded in my job. It never occurred to me that just because it was successful for them, it might not be successful for anyone else. Maybe – just as importantly – I never even considered that that team was having success *despite* what the coach was doing.

It wasn't until six months into my first head coaching position that I realised I could really influence how a team played on a match day with my training design and principles. I was fortunate that I was coaching a group of players who trusted me, and who were also able to take what I was asking them on the training ground and immediately apply it on match days. It was a real eureka moment! I'd accidentally discovered the concept of 'coaching periodisation'. I jumped in with both feet, and my improvement as a coach was immediate.

Relevance

To try to simplify things as much as possible, coaching periodisation (also known as tactical periodisation) is the concept of linking your training sessions back to your principles of play. It's a concept that was made popular in the mid-2000s when Jose Mourinho's Chelsea and Rafa Benitez's Liverpool regularly went head-to-head in some of the most fiercely contested battles of that era, and arguably sparked the greatest tactical advances in the Premier League. However, Mourinho and Benitez eventually became so obsessed with the concept of 'denying the opposition' that they had to disguise their methodology to mentally exhausted players.

What stuck with me, though, is the idea of making *everything* done at training relevant to what happens on match day and the team's principles of play. For the purposes of our training principles, there may be less of a focus on the tactical element and a greater focus on all aspects of the four-corner model. The aim being that when we design our practice, we're touching the physical, technical, tactical and psychological/social corners equally.

There are different levels to this. Obviously, 'phase of play' work on playing out from the back will have a clear and direct relevance to the players as to what you want on match day. However, those kinds of practices can be mentally fatiguing and have limited ball rolling time as you attempt to correct early failures.

At the other end of the spectrum, something as simple as bib tag can coach a principle like 'off-the-ball movement' with a much lighter touch. A more balanced practice might be a small-sided game that encourages players to break a line with a pass whilst playing away from pressure.

Overall, the aim is to make as much of your training session as relevant as possible to your match day principles. Obviously, you know your team better than anyone, and the skill for the coach is to design a practice that is appropriate to your players.

A phase of play practice might be too focused for under-11s, and bib tag might be too 'subtle' for a semi-pro men's team. It's about when to subtly reinforce those principles and when to really drive them home. What ultimately was the undoing for Benitez and Mourinho was the relentless intensity of their sessions; they eventually wore out their players both physically and mentally.

Is This Right For My Players?

In the beginning, like every coach, I thought I was doing fine and that I was changing the game forever. I would come up with incredibly complex and restrictive practices that looked amazing on paper but which would frustrate my players and fail to achieve their aims. Their frustration was only matched by my frustration! It took me a long time to understand the rationale for that, rather than dismissing it as a 'bad attitude'.

Now, whenever I look at a session plan, especially one I've not designed, there is always a first question I ask myself. (It wasn't until I started to develop my own coaching principles that I really started to reflect on my sessions and ask myself the question.) *Who is the session for?* My players or myself? In my early days as a coach, the reasons for my players' frustration was simple: my practice designs were "too complex", "too rigid", and "too slow" for players who got 60 minutes a week to play. I designed what I thought a good session should look like, and not what my players needed.

Ball Rolling Time

You're a new coach, fresh with enthusiasm and a great session planned. Some part of you wants this moment documented for historians to refer back to later. Part of you just wants to make sure that you get all your points across. You explain the practice and tell the players what you want. You tell them about the session layout, how to score, and what you're looking for them to achieve. You're talking… and talking… and talking. Players are looking at their boots; they've stopped listening, but still you talk.

Nothing kills a good session more than the coach's voice. I've seen really good sessions just murdered by a coach's constant intervention. Even when we have the best intentions, we can be harming our own session. On my level 2 assessment, for example, I put together my practice and took extra time to make sure every detail was in the players' minds. The session started, and it was a cold and very wet night, so I limited my interventions to ensure the players kept moving.

Pretty confident I'd done the right thing, and my session had been a good one, I was crushed when I was informed that my ball rolling time had been just 50%! I'd simply taken too long to get going, and despite minimal intervention, they'd literally spent half the practice listening to my voice.

The English FA and Wales FA both suggest 75-80% ball rolling time as the target within a session. If you're a coach with a 60-minute session, it can be really easy to get away from that target when you factor in warm up, setup time, water breaks and transitioning between practices.

On the flip side, "Don't forget to coach" was the advice given to me by that same tutor before I embarked on my UEFA B licence course. We all want to get our session moving, but there's nothing worse than irritated players trying to figure out the conditions because you've missed a vital point.

We can often feel guilty about stopping our practice too often, but in reality, that's what we are there for. When intervening in a practice, my aim is to limit my interventions to 60 seconds, so that I can get my points across clearly without losing the attention of the players and the intensity of the session. If I can combine this by coaching in blocks to give the players a breather, then it wastes even less time.

Setup Time

We all love to walk onto an empty practice pitch with the moveable goals exactly where we want them to be, and ample time to set up. Often, though, we're busy herding off the previous group whilst asking them (in vain) to move their multi-goal game setup off the pitch (to save doing it yourself).

We often have very little time in which to set up our practices. Practices that are overly complex, and which require a lot of equipment, often leave players standing on the sidelines waiting for you to start. When I was on my UEFA B assessment, two of the lads spent so much time putting down and moving cones that they ran out of time for the practice itself.

One method I like to use is to build out my practices within the same space. So, if I'm using a 35 by 25m space for the first practice and a 35 by 40m practice for my second practice, I will set up one practice inside the other and simply remove the cones as I go. Additionally, I'm very sparing with a cone. I will always try to use existing lines within a pitch to save me from marking out additional space.

Is The Space Easily Adjustable?

One of the benefits of using fixed lines already on the pitch is that it allows you to adjust the size a lot quicker. I'll be the first to admit that I'm terrible at judging space when it comes to practice setup.

When I first set out as a coach, I felt spaces had to be massive to really touch the physical corner. I didn't so much touch the physical corner but slapped it right in the face! This came to the detriment of the technical corner, and it wasn't until a recent reflection that I looked to make spaces smaller to increase the technical demands on my players. It created a different kind of intensity that still touched the physical corner.

Now, when I set up a practice, I plan to make sure that it is easily adjustable so that I can change the focus according to the needs of my players.

Is Everyone Moving?

I don't have many non-negotiables for new coaches when they join our club, but one of those non-negotiables is to keep everyone moving. Manchester in winter is cold, wet, and windy, and frequently all three.

As a result, I really hate to see practices where players are queuing to wait their turn to go; or their movements are so restricted that they're virtually static. In addition to creating bored, disinterested players, the sudden movements from static to movement in cold weather can often lead to unnecessary muscle injuries.

Can It Be Done With A Ball?

The second of my non-negotiables stems from the question: "Can it be done with a ball?" It was from one of my first opportunities as a coach that I picked up my second (and still strictest) coaching philosophy. Each week, we'd train for two hours, during which the Head Coach would 'run' the players for the first hour.

After 60 minutes of cross-country, I'd inherit exhausted, bored players who had little to no interest in listening to what I had to say as a coach, and who just wanted to get a ball moving to save a wasted evening.

Each week became an increasingly futile effort to coach players who didn't want to listen and were just keen to get a ball moving as quickly as possible. What that coach failed to realise was that the motivation for those players being there was to *play football*.

Conclusion

The considerations in this chapter are not exhaustive, and I'm sure that there will be things that you've factored into your practices that I've not listed above.

Going back to Rafa Benitez for a moment, in one of his very first sessions as Liverpool manager, he set his players off on a lap of the pitch. Halfway around, he called them back and told them never to do something again without first asking, "why?"

Aside from winning instant creditability with his players – who probably realised that their days of running laps were over – it was also an immediate challenge to ask them to open their minds and consider why they were doing something.

If we even begin to consider half of the above that we've gone through, then we're on our way to designing more effective practices for our players.

3. Playing Principles

In the previous chapter, we looked at some of the considerations that come into play when planning our training sessions. In this chapter, we will take a closer look at the *purpose* of a session and what we want our players to achieve within it.

What Are 'Principles of Play?'

In short, principles of play (or The Game Model) are the strategies a team uses to adapt to any situation during a game. At its most basic, as they will tell you on your English FA Level 1, football is an invasion game whose most fundamental strategies are to 'score a goal' whilst aiming 'to prevent the opponent from scoring'.

Most Game Models are broken down into the four moments of any given game:

- In Possession – What do we do when *we have the ball?*
- Defensive Transition – What do we do when *we first lose the ball?*
- Out of Possession – What do we do when *the opposition has the ball?*
- Attacking Transition – What do we do when *we win the ball back?*

Each of these principles works in conjunction with the others, and the game model is often presented in the below diagram.

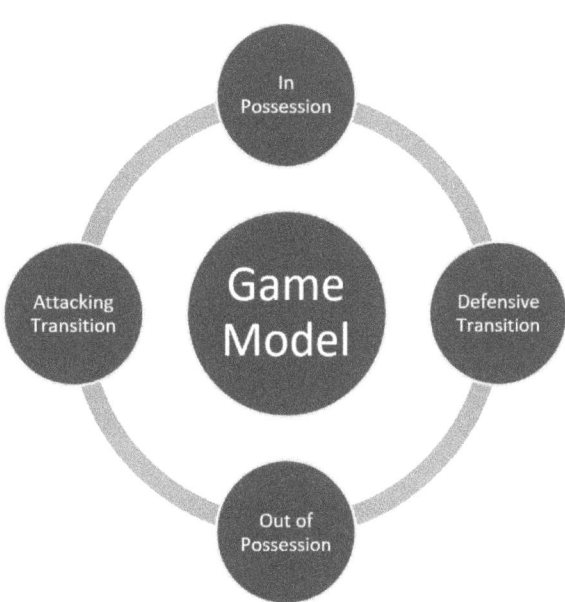

Naturally, the higher the level of football, the more likely a team's principles of play will have more detail and a narrower focus. At the very highest level, coaches like

Jose Mourinho and Pep Guardiola will have sub-principles to their principles, and in some extreme cases, even sub-principles to the sub-principles.

Where To Begin…

As coaches, it's often (but not always) on us to devise the 'principles' that we want our teams to play with, and creating your game model can be daunting for any new coach.

Fortunately, in recent years, national football associations have begun to define their own principles of play to help coaches, whilst providing a template for player development, as they look to create a more 'holistic' pathway for players.

Below are examples of the respective principles of play from the English FA and the Football Association of Wales. These principles are cascaded to any coaches who've attended a coaching course within the respective associations in recent years. These are known as 'England DNA' and 'The Welsh Way'.

The principal thinking in having these principles was to ensure that players are exposed to a 'playing identity' from age group football right through to their national teams. The idea is that if they're exposed to similar concepts at U12s through to U21s, then this will aid players in being able to compete on the international stage.

There was a secondary aim for the English FA, though, as they looked to move away from their own teachings of the 1980s. Back then, the director of coaching (Charles Hughes) authored the FA's own coaching manual, in which he stated that the most effective way to score goals was to get the ball into the opponent's penalty area with four passes or less.

Critics have since claimed that this philosophy led to a lost generation of players who lack basic technical skills and tactical understanding to compete at the highest level internationally.

In recent years, England's men's team have reached the finals of the European Championship, won the U21s European Championship and – famously – the women's team won the Women's European Championships at Wembley in 2022.

Likewise, since 2016, Wales have reached the semi-finals of the 2016 European Championships and qualified for the World Cup for the first time since 1958 in 2022.

As we will see, though, there are significant differences in the level of detail provided by the English and Welsh Associations.

ENGLAND DNA	
Attacking	**Defending**
Penetration	Press
Create Space	Delay
Movement	Cover & Balance
Support	Compactness
Creativity	Control & Restraint

England DNA is clear in its aims of what it wishes its teams to do in possession: to "penetrate", "create space", and offer "movement". However, the brevity of detail allows the coach to dig into the best way his or her team might achieve this; the coach can create their own sub-principles relevant to their team's needs.

For example, one coach might decide that the best way for their team to build up from the back is to play out through the centre-backs; another coach might feel it's best for their team to go long. The onus is on the coach to decide what is best for their players and apply that to their practices.

The FA encourages the 'narrowing of topics' when a coach is considering their session design. For example, a practice to break lines might be narrowed to "Breaking lines by receiving in the half-space through central areas".

There is no mention of transitions. This is because, in the early courses, learners were asked to think about the following when constructing their session designs: "Does it look like a game?" As a result, when putting together a practice with either an attacking or defending focus, there will *naturally* be elements of transition in the practice.

The Welsh Way has greater specificity and a narrower focus on its playing principles. This gives coaches and players greater clarity and definition of their aims and how they wish for them to be achieved. In turn, this will create a stronger identity in playing style amongst its teams.

For example, "Clear decision-making to play through, round, over" is clear that all three options can be applied, and that the onus is on the coach to ensure that the decision-making process remains with the players.

Welsh Way	
In Possession	**Attacking Transition**
<ul><li>Confidence to take the ball</li><li>Clear decision-making to play through, round, over</li><li>Move the ball quickly – find the spare player</li><li>Create and exploit scoring opportunities</li></ul>	<ul><li>Anticipate the transition</li><li>Secure the first pass</li><li>Play forward early</li><li>Support quickly</li><li>Move into an attacking shape</li></ul>
Defensive Transition	**Out of Possession**
<ul><li>Anticipate the transition</li><li>Fast pressure on the ball</li><li>Stop forward passes</li><li>Force away from goal</li><li>Recover quickly into defensive shape</li></ul>	<ul><li>Show away from goal</li><li>Block central passes</li><li>Stop switches of play</li><li>Protect the space between the lines</li><li>Control the space behind the first line</li></ul>

The strength of these two game models is that they are designed with grassroots football in mind and can be comfortably applied, regardless of your level of the game.

The English FA have freely admitted that in designing their DNA, they have 'borrowed' large elements from the Spanish, Germans and Dutch to create a blend of their own. Meanwhile, the Welsh FA are clear in their desire to produce more technicians like Gareth Bale and Joe Allen.

Designing Your Own

It took me a long time to think about how I wanted to influence my players, both on the training pitch and in matches. Even when I started to form strong beliefs about how I wanted my teams to play, it took some time before I began to put everything down on paper.

Everyone wants to press like a peak Jurgen Klopp Liverpool, or pass in beautiful triangles like Pep Guardiola's 2012 Barcelona. There's not a coach alive who wouldn't love to have their name synonymous with a particular style of playing successful football (I'm sure Sam Allardyce and Sean Dyche are both proud of the fact that they're associated with their more direct styles of play, too!).

However, many things may define your principles of play, including (but not limited to) your personal footballing philosophy, the needs of your players, and potentially the culture of your club.

Identifying The Needs Of Your Players

When I arrived at the University of Manchester, my first consideration for how I wanted my team to play was, 'Were the players capable of playing it?' There's very little to be gained from implementing a style of football that the players are ill-suited to playing. Are you going to be able to implement an aggressive and complicated system if you've only an hour a week to work with your players?

For me, it was crucial to ensure the playing style accentuated the strengths of the players whilst protecting their weaknesses. In my first season, one of our two biggest strengths was our technical ability and our capability to take on information and apply it. On the flip side, although we were a team of fast, agile and physically fit players, we were up against players who were much stronger than us physically.

As a result, I designed our principles to be almost a form of evasion when in possession; to make the pitch as big as possible and to seek to play around the press to prevent the opponent from physically dominating us. When out of possession, we aimed to win the ball as high up the field as we could, using our speed as a means to disrupt the rhythm of the opponent's desire to settle on the ball. These were among my first principles of play.

It is worth pointing out that these were ultra-narrow in their focus. As playing principles, they didn't leave a lot of clarity for other areas of the pitch.

We couldn't just have those two principles of play, of course, or else we would have become a one-dimensional side incapable of playing in other areas of the field or with any understanding of what to do when not in these two scenarios.

Culture Club

Another (and equally important) question I asked myself was, 'Would the players enjoy it?' As 'pay-to-play' players, there is very little reward if you walk off the pitch at the end of 90 minutes – having slogged through a game – and you can count the number of times you've touched the ball on one hand. It was important to recognise that playing a style of football that was enjoyable for the players to play was more important than what style of football I wanted to coach.

It took time to develop and evolve what worked for us as a team. Eventually, I settled on the following that I felt would tick all the boxes for us as a team:

UMWFC Principles of Play	
In Possession	**Transition Out of Possession**
<ul><li>Make the pitch as big as we can</li><li>Attack the space created</li><li>Play the safest, most direct pass</li><li>Find the free player</li><li>Play around or through the press</li></ul>	<ul><li>Initial pressure around the ball</li><li>Prevent or delay the counter-attack</li><li>Force away from our goal</li><li>Recover our shape</li><li>Make the space compact</li></ul>
Transition into Possession	**Out of Possession**
<ul><li>Protect the ball</li><li>Play away from pressure</li><li>Can we play forwards quickly?</li><li>Passing options for the ball carrier</li><li>Start the counter-attack</li></ul>	<ul><li>Remain as compact as possible</li><li>Leave the furthest player</li><li>Protect the middle of the field</li><li>Let the opposition play in safe areas</li><li>Make the opposition's play predictable</li></ul>

Understanding

One of the things that I wanted to ensure was that I tailored my language so that all the players had a clear understanding of their meaning. A crucial mistake we can make as coaches is to assume that our players know what we mean when we use technical terms or jargon. This can be overcome by being consistent with our language and checking players' understanding at regular intervals.

Communication is a critical aspect for us, as coaches. The reality is that unless you're working in a professional environment, it's unlikely that you're going to have your players in a classroom for hours at a time, breaking down the minute details of how you want them to play.

If you're lucky, you might have a meeting at the start of the season in which you can lay out the foundations of how you wish to play. However, if you're coaching a very young age group, then how much are they likely to take in, or what interest are they likely to have?

It's really crucial that we understand how we are going to get our messages across to our players. It's also important to understand that different approaches work for different players/teams.

Once, I was observing a session with our third team when I was asked to manage the defending team for the coach. The coach's focus was on attacking in the final third, whilst his defenders were left to try and prevent that attack. Initially, there was confusion and a lack of cohesion in the defensive unit, allowing the attacking team to have early success in front of goal.

During a break, I gathered the players to check their understanding of what was expected of them. What I discovered was that there was a significant difference in the level of understanding of their football knowledge and tactical experience.

Together, we came up with some simple command words for how we wanted the players to defend, using "baguette" when we wanted the players to stay in a compact line, and "banana" when we wanted the back line to bend and push out a full-back to put pressure on the ball.

It was a turning point in the session as the attacking players were suddenly challenged with a much more realistic defensive line; the now-motivated defending unit had great fun shouting "Baguette" or "Banana" amidst confused-looking attackers. That basic understanding gave them a clear and unified purpose, and they quickly went from defending as individuals to a solid defensive unit.

It was a rudimentary way of communicating between players – developed in the moment – but as long as your players are able to understand, there is no incorrect way to successfully implement understanding.

What Does Success Look Like?

Football is a challenging and complex sport where success is measured differently depending on the expectations of the individual club. Pep Guardiola is not just assessed on whether he wins a trophy but on *how many* trophies he wins. If we applied that same measure to every other coach in the country, then 99.9% of coaches are going to have failed seasons.

The same applies to players during games, too. If your principle is to build up through the thirds and your measure of success is 'to score a goal', then you're going to fail almost 100% of the time and find yourself with frustrated and demotivated players. When implementing anything new, it is vital to have a clear understanding of what early success looks like and to have an increasing scale of what success is to your players.

I once worked with a coach who coached his players to get rid of the ball in their defensive third as quickly as possible, regardless of the outcome after possession was surrendered. In an attempt to retain better control of possession, I attempted to implement a more patient build-up style of play for the team. Yet, after just a few sessions, the manager reverted back to what he knew because 'it wasn't working'.

The manager thought it was going to be like flipping a switch; expecting his players to carve open all before him after a session or two. One of my failures as a coach, in this instance (with the manager), was to fail to agree or identify what different levels of success looked like.

In a perfect world, the goalkeeper would play the ball out to the centre-back, and half a dozen passes later, is celebrating a goal from the perfect attack. Sadly, that's not the sport we love, and when I began to coach on my own for the first time, I had to demonstrate what different levels of success looked like to ensure people bought into what we were trying to achieve.

Early on, we had a clear measure of what success looked like when playing out from the back. Conceding a throw-in on halfway was still a success because we had better field position, and were in a 'safer' area of the field. Likewise, winning a throw-in 20 yards from our goal was still considered a success because we retained possession of the ball, and this allowed us to make the space we played in bigger.

Just as important was the need not to get disheartened by early failures. Too often, as coaches, when something doesn't work, we can be very quick to abandon the plan. In each case, above, progress was made, and by getting the players to recognise the 'quick wins', I was able to get a much stronger buy-in to our playing principles.

Review And Reflect

It's important to stress that a team's principles of play can be a living, breathing thing that evolves as your team does. Once you've written them down on paper, it does not mean they are then set in stone.

In 'The Mixer', an excellent book about the evolution of tactics across the first 20 years of the Premier League, author Michael Cox often talks about how Sir Alex Ferguson reflected on his experiences of playing sides in Europe to adjust his side's tactics in the Premier League. They were one of the first sides to stop playing a 4-4-2 and adopted a shape with one striker, so they were better equipped to go far in Europe.

Ferguson, whose early sides were famed for their attacking wing play, wasn't afraid to change what he knew in the search for better long-term results. United fans at the time decreed it was 'too defensive' when the reality was Ferguson – due to his

European exposure – had a clear idea of what the future of the game looked like, far ahead of his domestic rivals.

For me, the very nature of university football accepts a high turnover of players over a three-year period. And this forces regular reflections on our playing principles. As the personnel change and the characteristics of the team change, (we've no scope for recruitment), then the football principles need reviewing and potentially tweaking.

For you, devising your own (or even adopting your own football association's) principles of play will help provide your training sessions with far greater definition and clarity.

4. The Build Up Phase

"The intention is not to move the ball,
rather to move the opposition."

Pep Guardiola

It was minutes before the kick-off of my very first game as a head coach, and my goalkeeper chose that very moment to inform me of something unexpected. They would form my first playing principle as a coach.

"I can't kick the ball off the ground."

What followed was 45 minutes of my goalkeeper doing her best to take goal kicks as my three centre-backs took turns to try and win 50/50 headers at the edge of the penalty area. They all probably wondered how I'd even got the job (the other guy didn't show up for the interview), but to their credit, we made it to half-time only 2-0 down.

Luckily for me, that 45 minutes bought me enough time to produce a plan for the second half. I positioned two of my centre-backs around the six-yard box, looking to invite the press centrally and then play around it. All things considered, a 3-0 defeat wasn't a reflection of the game from the second half showing; indeed, we created a number of chances but were met by some inspired goalkeeping from a future Tiktok celebrity. It was a sobering experience, but I learned more in 90 minutes of football than I had in the previous two years of coaching.

This match produced my first footballing principle… that we needed to be able to play out from the back. Since that day, I've coached my sides to build up from the goalkeeper not only as a necessity for the team's needs, but also as a more enjoyable way for my players to play. The last thing I want for my players is to come off and count the number of touches they've had in a game on one hand.

Coaching players to build up from the back can be a very daunting process for a grassroots coach as early setbacks can knock not only the players' confidence but the coach's too. I was extremely fortunate that I had the early buy-in from my players.

Initially, I felt it was important to set measures for success for the players – so that we could gradually build up our confidence. At first, success was considered to play the ball away from our penalty area, even if it meant defending a throw-in just outside of it. As a team, we agreed that this was a safer area to defend, and we backed ourselves to defend a throw-in.

As we grew in confidence, we aimed to retain possession and be more successful in breaking lines to move the ball up the field. Eventually, we were confident enough to move the ball as a means of launching attacks.

The seminal moment came a couple of games in, when we were faced with playing on a tight, narrow grass pitch without much room to play with the centre-backs; we had to create as much depth as possible to find time on the ball to either switch play or break a line. An 11-minute hat-trick from our left winger – in which possession had started either from our centre-back or goalkeeper – cemented our playing identity. Since then, it has become a fundamental playing principle for all of my teams.

Following on from the previous chapter, where we identified our principles of play, we shall now add some sub-principles based on the area of the pitch that we find ourselves in.

Our in possession principles:

- Make the pitch as big as we can
- Attack the space created
- Play the safest, most direct pass
- Find the free player
- Play around or through the press

Our four additional sub-principles – for when we want to build up from our goalkeeper – are:

1. Move the ball away from our goal
2. Play away from pressure
3. Break a line
4. Maintain the ability to switch the play

Making The Pitch As Big As We Can

The first thing we looked to do was make the pitch as big as possible for ourselves and create gaps in the opponent's press. It's these gaps that we want to exploit and play in. This is done by our wingers and full-backs pulling out to the wing to make the pitch as *wide* as possible. This immediately forces the opposition to cover more space when defending and creates space in which to pass through their press.

Equally, *depth* is critical as we want to force the opposition to leave gaps between their lines, which will allow us to receive the ball in space. It was also crucial that our shape is *balanced* so the opposition cannot create overloads or cover multiple players with one defender.

In Figure 1, I've chosen a goal kick as it provides us with a scenario where we are the furthest point from our goal (playing from bottom to top) and both sides are balanced in their shape. We are set up in a 4-3-3 with a single pivot.

Our outside attackers ❼ are as high as possible, our centre-backs ❺ / ❹ are as deep as possible, and our full-backs ❸ / ❷ as wide as possible (to move the ball away from our goal). The aim of this is to try to isolate the opposition's front line, forcing them to widen, which allows us to play through their press.

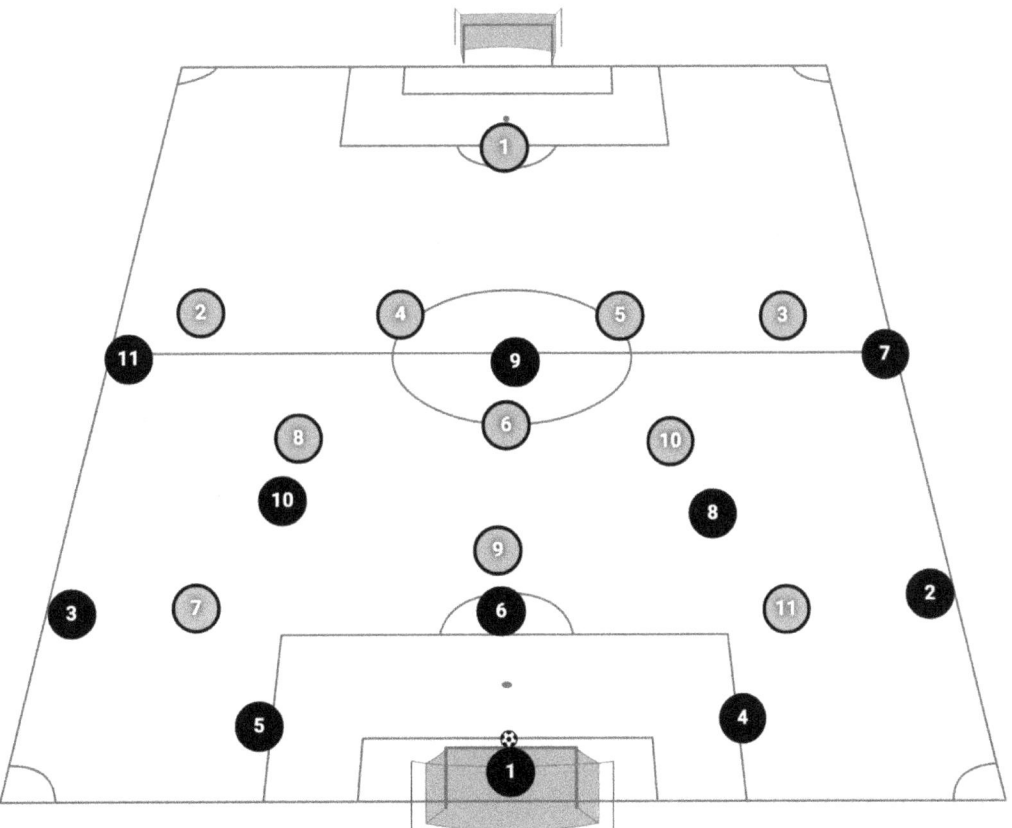

Figure 1 – Goal Kick; opposition balanced.

Play The Safest, Most Direct Pass

When we are in possession in our own third, we are always looking to make the most direct pass possible to move the ball away from danger. We do not wish to surrender possession in this section of the field as the opposition will have a high probability of creating an attacking opportunity.

The initial setup of our shape should allow the centre-back in possession to make a forward pass inside to the centre midfielder ❽ or outside to the full-back ❷ (to play away from pressure). When the goalkeeper ❶ or centre-back is in possession, we want to ensure that they have passing options to play forwards or to play away from the goal/opposition's press.

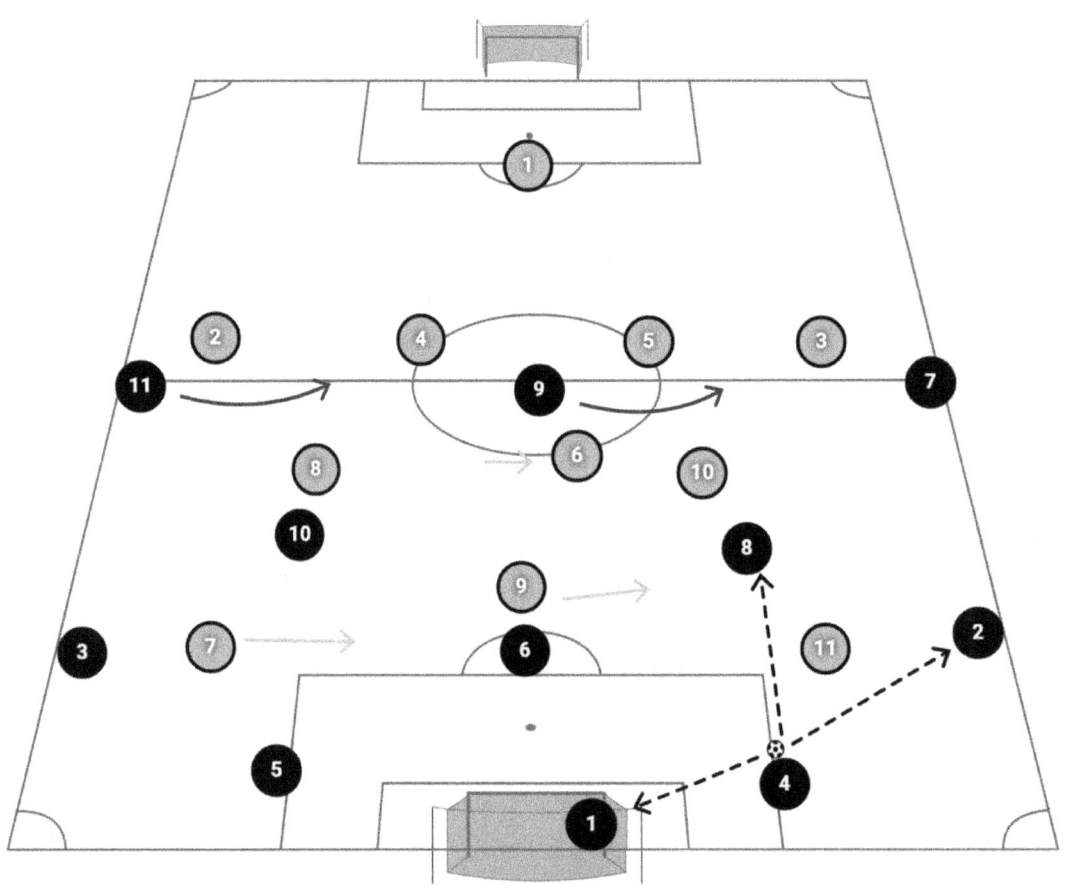

Figure 2 – Centre-back in possession.

We are happy to play to our full-backs as it is difficult for the opponents to create overloads on them, and because we can bring the touchline into play. If they are unable to play a forward pass, then the goalkeeper becomes a passing option to switch the play.

Often, our first pass to a centre-back triggers movement (Figure 2) as we try to exploit space or create an overload. In this example, centre forward ❾ is looking to occupy the gap between the opposition centre-back and full-back, which has been created by the winger pulling as wide as they can.

Attack The Space Created

When we are successful in breaking a line through the opposition into central areas (Figure 3), we want to try to break a second line in turn. This is ideally done by making a pass into the space between the opposition's midfield or defensive lines. Alternatively, we would look to play a pass behind the opposition's back line. If we are unable to play forwards, we are still able to play away from pressure as the full-back remains in space.

If the opposition remain narrow and we're unable to play through their press, we aim to play around or over it (Figure 3). In this instance, the outside centre midfielder looks to play in behind the opposition back line.

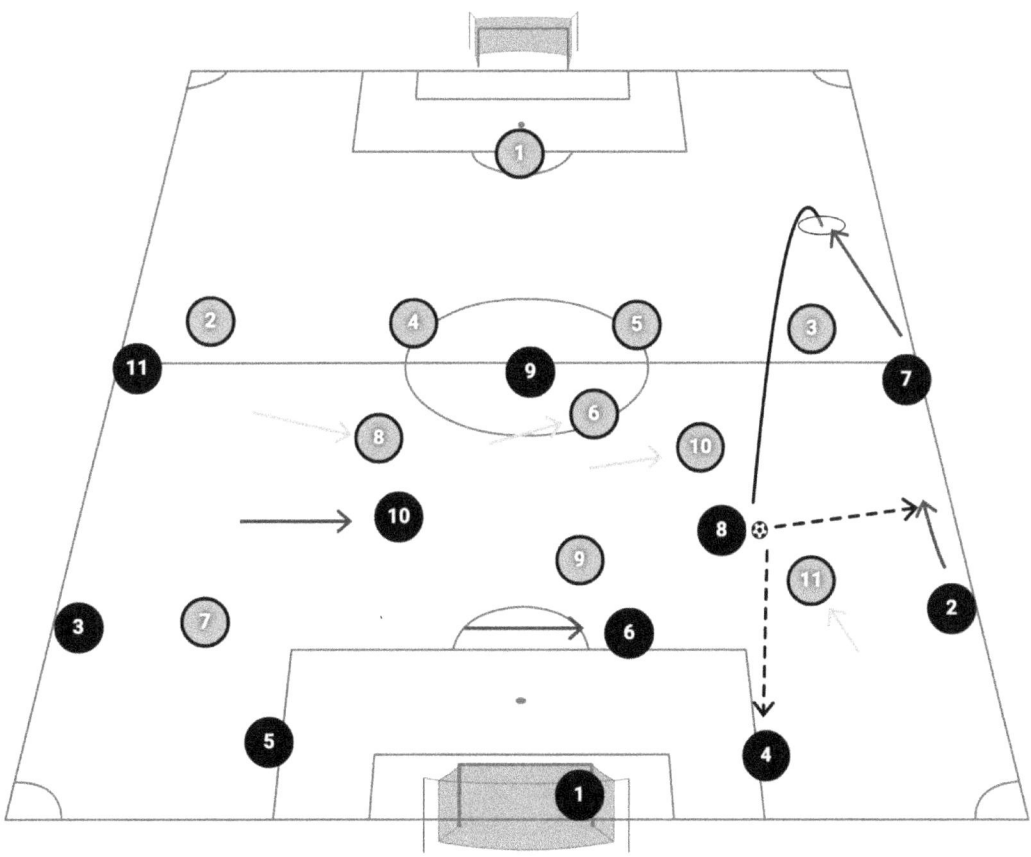

Figure 3 – Outside centre midfielder in possession.

Pep Guardiola will often talk about how breaking a line with consecutive passes is the most damaging thing for any defending team, as it will leave the defensive line exposed.

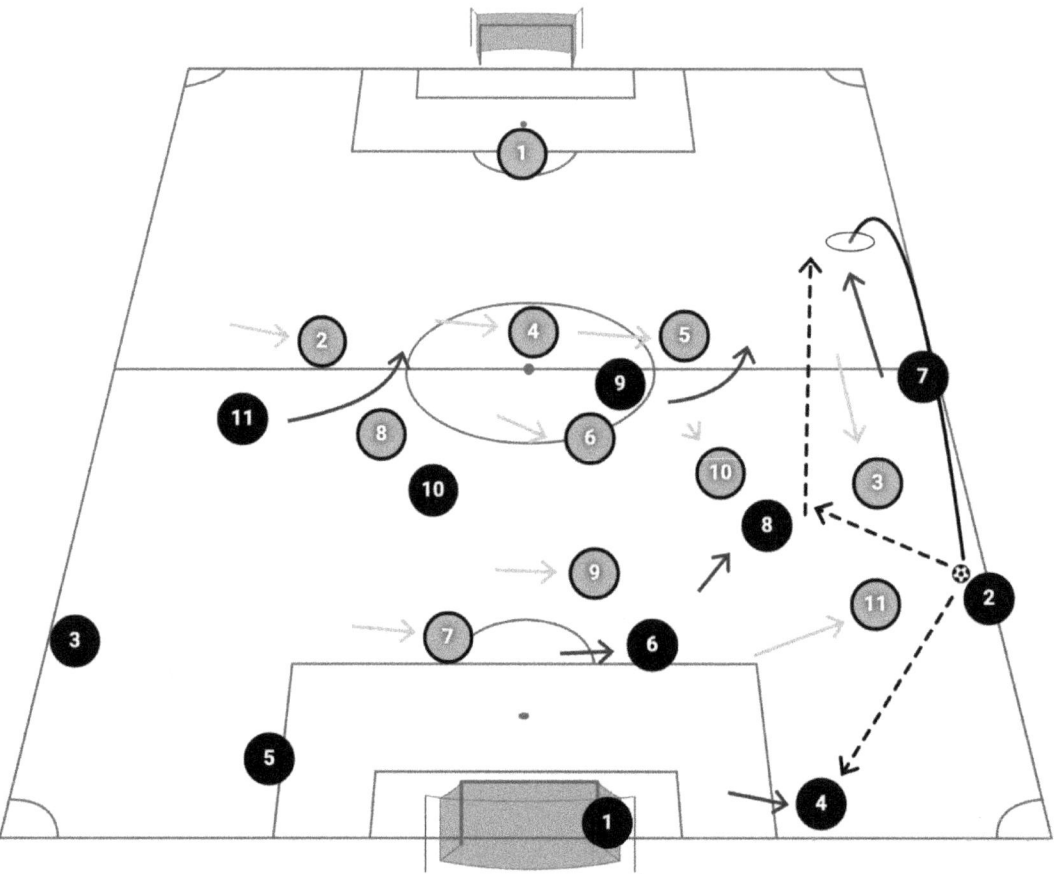

Figure 4 – Full-back in possession.

Play Around Or Through The Press

If the opponent prevents us from moving the ball forwards, it is critical that the centre-backs remain deep to invite the switch of play (Figure 5). If the centre-backs advance with the ball, then the opposition will be able to force us into pressing traps. When the centre-backs remain deep, the opposition's forward line is forced into a decision over whether or not to break their defensive shape.

If the opposition remain in their shape, the back line has time to receive and switch the ball. If the forwards follow them, this allows our midfield ❻ to drop into the space to receive the ball inside. When we switch the ball, it is crucial we still look to break a line.

The key for all three options is to retain control of the ball in safe areas where, if we are dispossessed, we have numbers behind the ball and are away from the middle of the pitch. Just as importantly, the decision-making process stays with the players on the field as our practices allow them to decide what the safest way to beat the opposition block is.

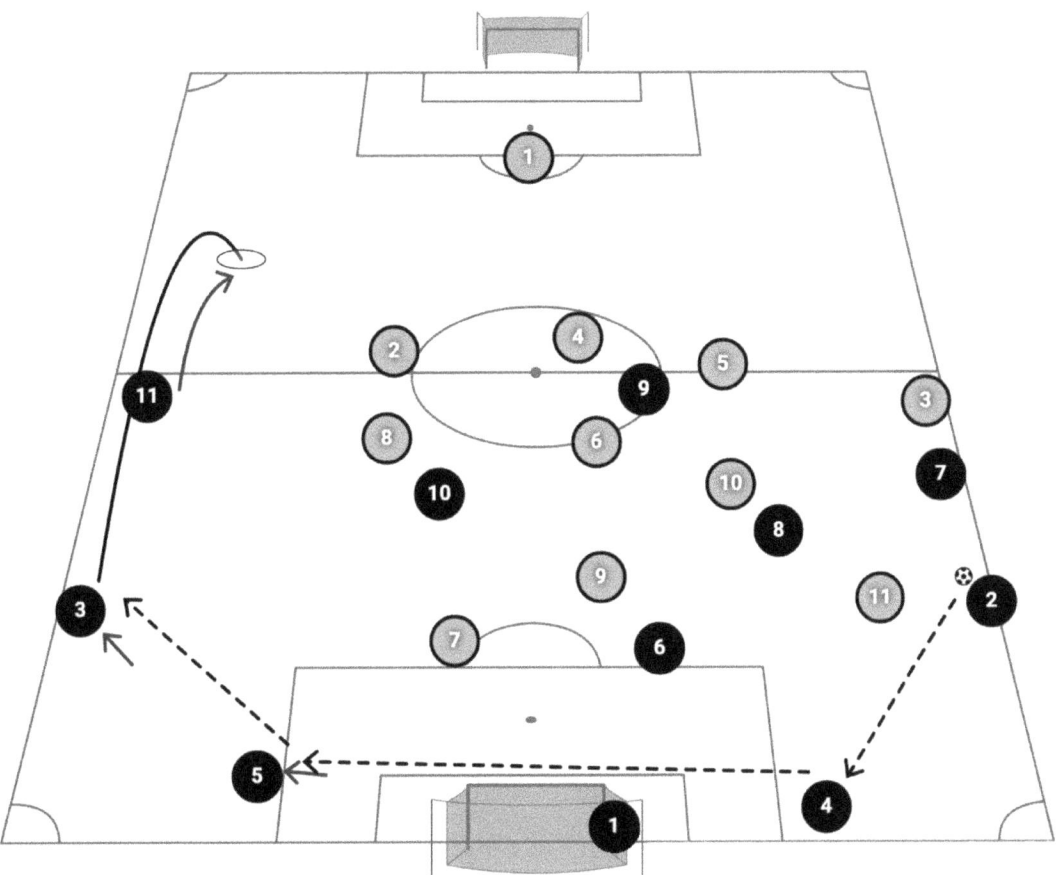

Figure 5 – Centre-backs dropping to invite the switch of play.

Conclusion

Now that we have identified how we want to build out from the back as a team, the next step is to combine this with our training principles to create sessions that will allow us to achieve this. You will find these in Chapter 6. It's important to recognise that *how* you build up from the back is entirely up to you and what is best for your players. You may wish to play through your opponent or over them, as that is what suits your team's needs best. Having the context of *how* you wish to play will not only help you with your session design, but help provide your players with the context they need in those practices. Okay, onwards to Chapter 5!

5. Defending In The Attacking Third

"If you win the ball back high up the pitch, and you are close to the goal, a really good opportunity is only one pass away most of the time."

Jurgen Klopp

When we think about pressing in the final third, most of us will immediately think about either Jurgen Klopp's Borussia Dortmund or Liverpool teams as the gold standard of pressing.

As fans, it's easy to appreciate a side that presses aggressively high up the field as it directly mirrors our desire (as supporters) to see sides giving their all for the team we follow. I remember, as a teenager, seeing opposition teams aggressively press and wondering, "Why can't *my* side show that level of desire?"

I used to admire the Everton teams of the mid-00s with players like Andy Johnson, Marcus Bent and James Beattie, who would put the hard yards in for their team and prevent the opposition from settling on the ball.

It's as coaches that we realise the complexities that come with an aggressive press. The rewards of a high press cannot be understated; putting immediate pressure on the ball allows possession to be immediately won back near the opponent's goal. It allows for pressing traps to be set up in front of goal to create favourable goalscoring opportunities.

However, there are risks to a high press, such as the need for a high defensive line, and the importance of closing space quickly. It also requires much higher physical demands of players.

When I first started as a Head Coach, the first defending principles of my sides were based on the speed we possessed in the attacking third. Because of our lack of physicality, I wanted to utilise that speed to regain the ball in dangerous areas and prevent the opposition from being allowed to settle on the ball whilst keeping it as far away from our goal as possible.

However, pressing in the final third doesn't mean you must press like Jurgen Klopp's finest teams. As my team evolved and we became physically stronger, we sacrificed some of that speed, so we sat slightly deeper to protect the space behind our attacking lines.

Instead of our speed, we used our positioning to create pressing traps to win the ball back in deeper central areas, meaning that our defensive units remained compact right up until possession was regained.

A reminder of our out of possession principles:

- Remain as compact as possible
- Leave the furthest player
- Protect the middle of the field
- Let the opposition play in safe areas
- Make the opposition's play predictable

In this chapter, we look to add the following sub-principles:

1. Retain a balanced defensive shape
2. Cover space to invite the press
3. Protect the area in front of the defensive unit
4. Prevent the opposition from switching play
5. Set pressing traps

Remain As Compact As Possible

It's crucial – when out of possession – that we try to make the space between the lines as compact as possible and prevent our opponent from dropping in between them to receive the ball. The very best players thrive on being able to receive the ball between the lines on the half-turn. Players like David Silva thrive on the defender's hesitation to follow or leave their man, and use it to their full advantage to wreak havoc.

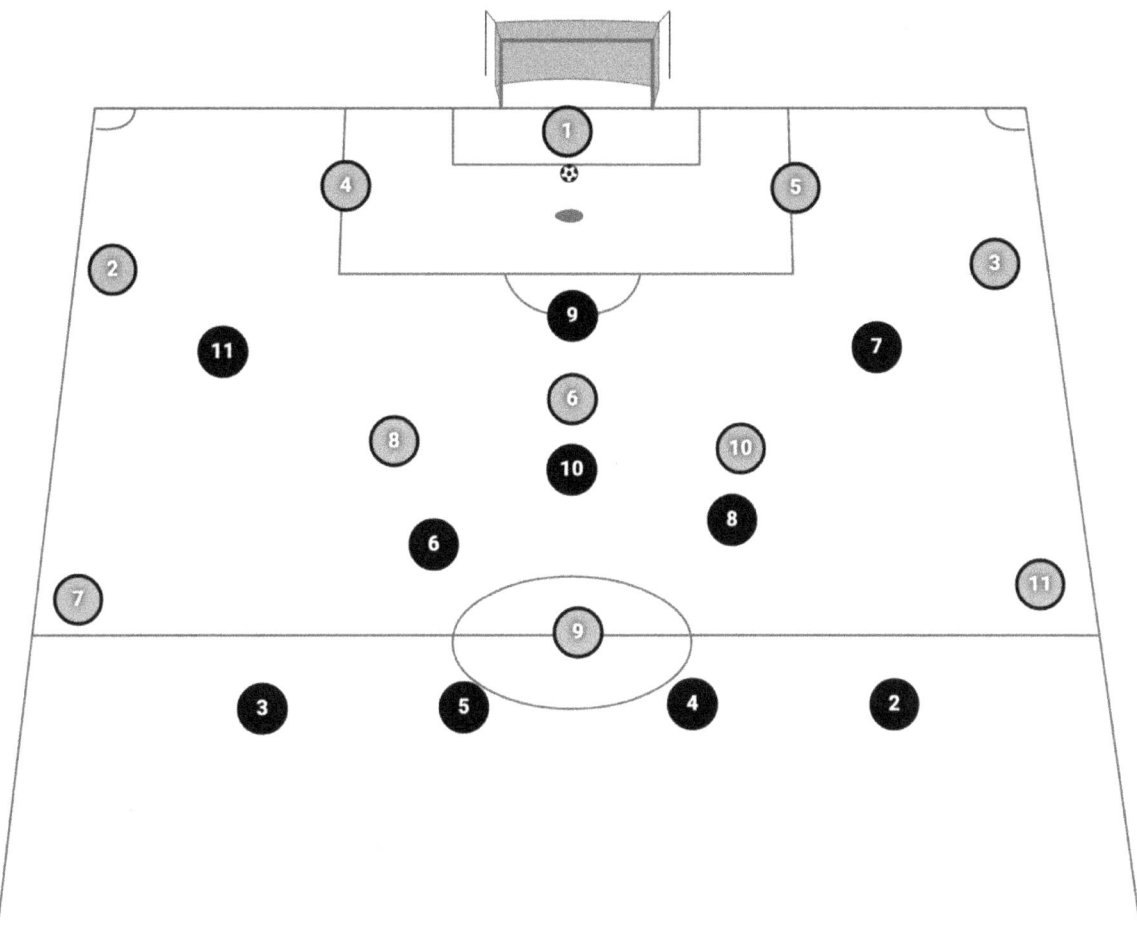

Figure 1 – Opposition Goal kick. Both teams balanced.

When the ball is in central areas, it is vital to remain as balanced as possible (Figure 1) because if we are unbalanced, it simply encourages the opposition to play away from pressure to where we are underloaded and create an overload for themselves.

At the same time, remaining as compact as possible allows us to adjust to what the opposition do without overcommitting. We want to make sure there is as small a space between our lines as possible. The opposition's first pass is often the trigger for our press and determining our actions. If we're over-aggressive, it can be a signpost to the opposition of what we're trying to do and how to beat our press.

Leave The Furthest Player

When pressing and looking to put pressure on the ball carrier, we have to consider which players are the immediate danger(s) to the situation. We must apply an appropriate amount of pressure to the player in possession and the players around the ball, whilst providing cover. If we're too aggressive, then the players behind us may not be in position to cover; if we're too slow, then the ball carrier has time to pick their pass.

It's also important that we consider what is happening away from the ball and look to provide cover for the secondary passes. As a team, we are looking to defend with at least one more player than the opposition attacks with, so we must consider which players we leave; in this instance, we're looking to leave the furthest players from the ball.

So, if we allow the first pass to go from centre to full-back, then we would leave the winger on the opposite side of the field free (Figure 2). We do this accepting that if the opponent is successful in switching the play, or able to hit a long diagonal ball, we'd have enough time and cover to regroup on the opposite side of the field and protect that area of the field.

One of the things that we want to make sure that we do is cover the player rather than tightly mark him. Pep Guardiola (that man again) often speaks about pressing space rather than marking the player because if a player is tightly marked, the ball carrier simply won't pass to him. Instead, we cover the space to invite the pass and then put the player under pressure.

Some teams will attempt to go player-for-player across the whole of the pitch. Indeed, Brentford are a great example of this when they won at the Etihad in November 2022. This was, in part, by shutting Manchester City down and preventing them from playing their normal passing game – matching them up player-for-player across the field. However, you must consider the physical and mental demands that this requires of your players.

Protect The Middle Of The Field

It's important that we always block the most direct route to goal. Nothing hurts a press like having central players getting sucked out into wide areas and leaving central areas unprotected and the opposition playing through them. When the ball is in central areas, we need to use our central players ❻ / ❽ / ❿ to protect those areas and provide cover should the opposition break a line with a direct pass.

It's equally important that – should a pass go into a wide area and the outside centre midfielder ❿ / ❽ goes out to press in that area, and the pivot moves across to cover – the far side centre midfielder comes across to protect the area in front of the centre-backs. We look to press the area in which the ball resides, cover the area around the ball, and protect the areas away from the ball to ensure that we are not hurt by multiple direct passes.

Former Manchester United Assistant Manager Rene Meulensteen would often talk about how the midfield must always protect the zone in front of the opposition back four at all times. The midfield unit must work in tandem to only leave the space when it has been occupied by another midfielder.

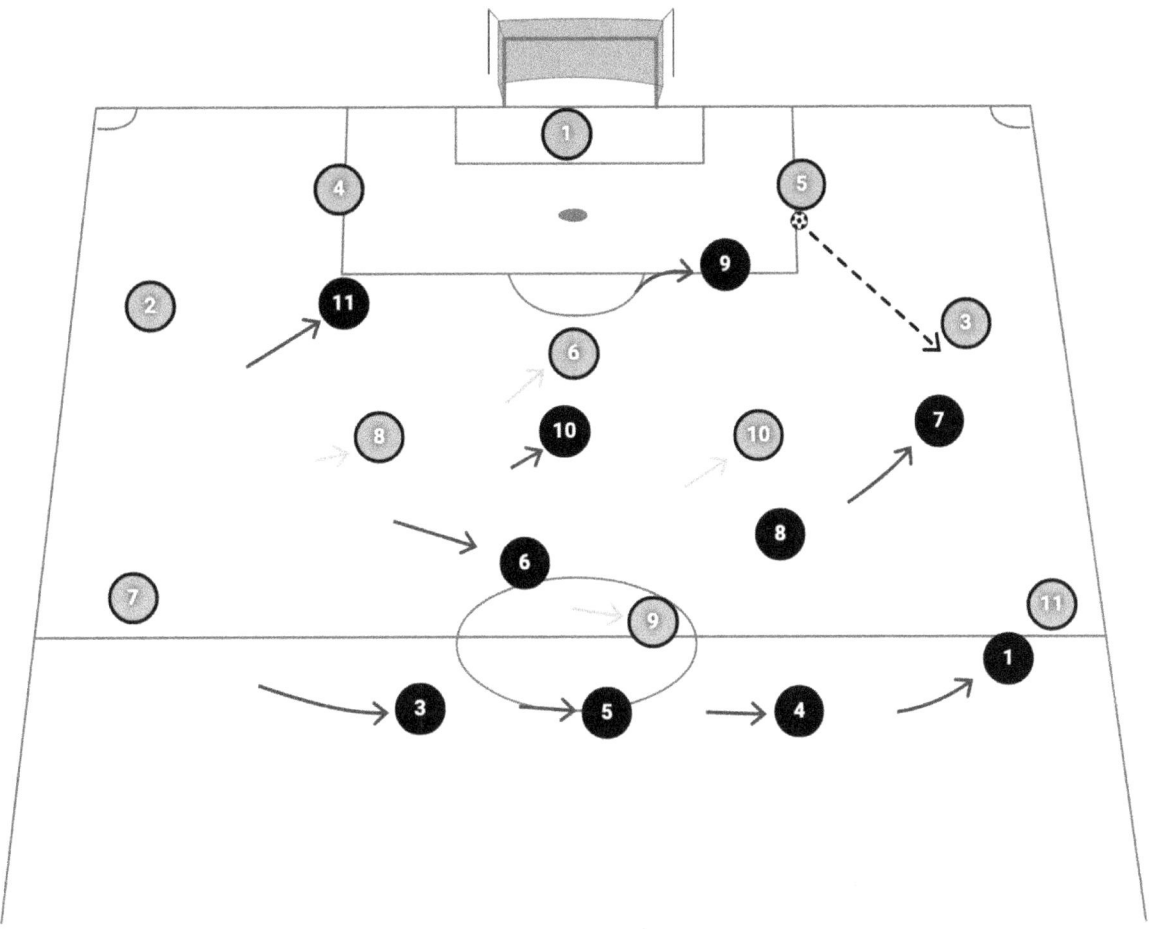

*Figure 2 – Centre-back in possession.
Defenders looking to stop the forward pass.*

Let The Opposition Play In Safe Areas

One of the things that we have to accept when we walk onto the field is that the opposition are going to have the ball at some point. However, there are areas where we are happy to let them play, one of which is around their own penalty area.

Whether the opposition are looking to play through the thirds and build out from their own goalkeeper, or hit it long, it's crucial that we don't step out of our own block and provide space behind our press for them to exploit.

If the goalkeeper or centre-backs are in possession when we're in our shape, then the ability to hurt us is reduced, provided our defensive block moves in time with the ball.

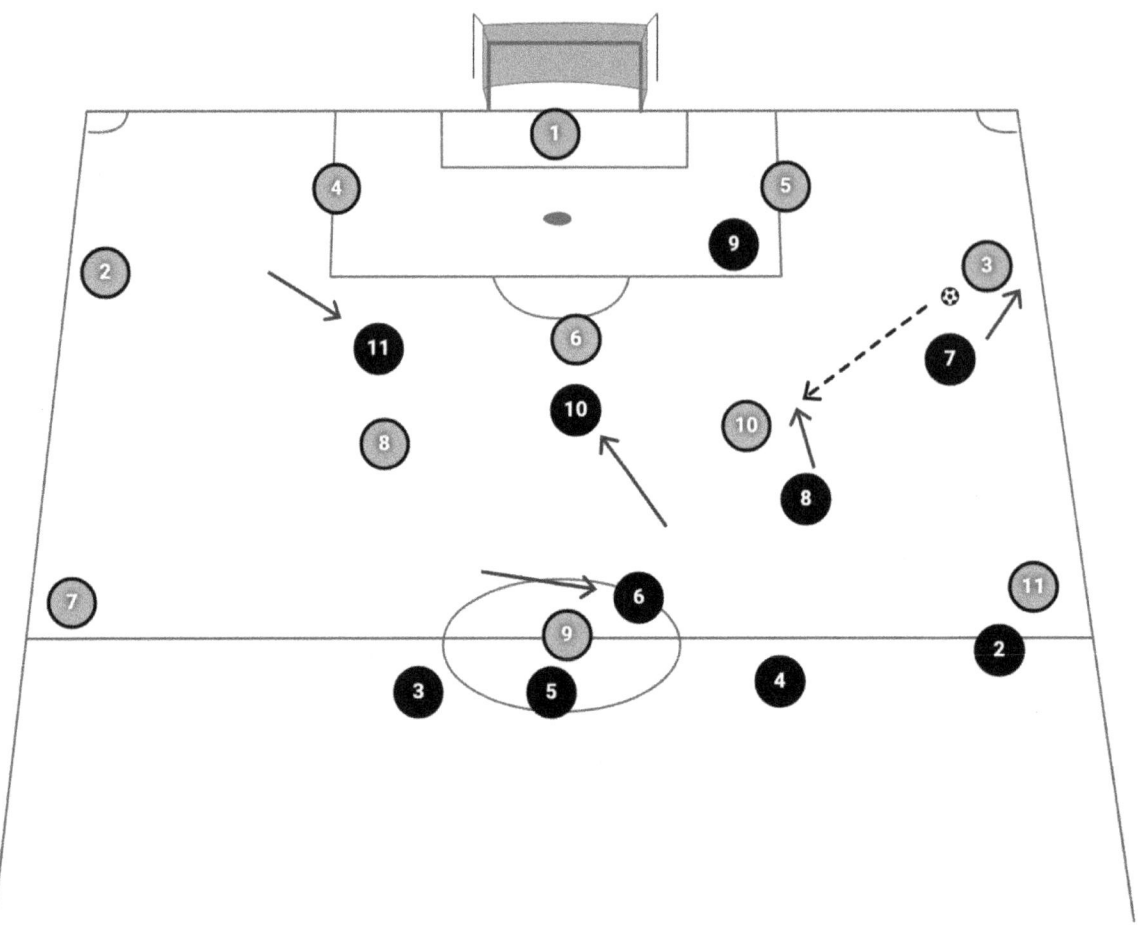

*Figure 3 – Full-back in possession.
Defenders looking to force the pass inside.*

Make The Opposition's Play Predictable

As mentioned above, Guardiola often talks about *pressing the space rather than the player*, with the rationale being that by tightly marking a player, that player is less likely to receive possession. This provides players with the opportunity to pinch the ball from unsuspecting defenders.

One of the additional advantages is that by pressing space and angling those runs, you aim to limit the number of passing options for the possession team and prevent them from breaking lines.

If the centre forward presses the inside of the centre-back but cuts across the forward pass into midfield, then they can direct the ball out to the full-back. Alternatively, they can angle their run across the central defender to force them to play away from goal, preventing the switch and 'cutting off' half of the pitch.

A 4-3-3 is vulnerable to forward passes in wide areas. If the winger ❼ works in tandem with the forward ❾ and angles their run to press the outside of the full-back, this can force the pass back inside.

In the first instance, this prevents the defender playing a direct pass, it allows us to delay the opposition's attack, and gives us time to get players behind the ball. This, in turn, forces the opponent from being able to play forwards and only allows them to play sideways or backwards.

If we take this further, this also allows us to set pressing traps to intercept the ball higher up the field and in front of the opponent's goal (Figure 3). With three central midfielders, we are strongest centrally and can thus set areas in which the midfielders can trap the opposition, attempt to win the ball back, and create scoring opportunities.

Conclusion

Pressing in the final third doesn't require you to have peak Luis Suarez/Lionel Messi/Neymar in your front three, but it's important to consider the players that you have *before* considering how you wish to press.

Since Borussia Dortmund and Barcelona revived the modern concept of high pressing, many sides have adjusted how they press to suit the demands and needs of their teams. More often now, especially in the Premier League, teams will use a high press as a means of delaying the opponent from quick counter-attacks rather than as a means of aiming to win the ball back.

Whatever your approach, the key to making a press successful is organising your shape to play to your team's defensive strengths. We will look at the coaching points for this in Chapter 6.

6. Build-Up Third – Practices

In this chapter, we look at the practices for the build up phase and attacking third areas of the pitch. Each of these practices has been designed so that the coach can focus on the build up phase when in possession and a high press when out of possession. The coaching points differ throughout with some focused on in possession, some out of possession, and some with both. The aim of these points is to provide guidance and demonstrate how they are linked with the previous chapters. These coaching points can be amended, depending on the aims and needs of the players. A reminder that the same practice can have many different coaching points based on your needs.

Key

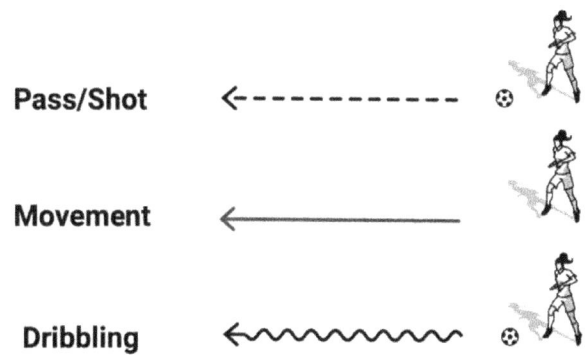

Reminders

- Throughout these practices, where I have included goalkeepers, this is to demonstrate how they can be used in the practice. If there are no goalkeepers, then they can be substituted for a mini goal or gate with a condition such as a 'two touch finish'.
- I have used the same number of players throughout the practices for uniformity, but have designed them so they can be adjusted for 8-18 players. If you are working with an odd number of players, working with a neutral player or 'magic player' should not impact the realism of the practice too greatly.
- Where I have used multiple goals or poles, this is to demonstrate the target that players are aiming to play to or through. Where mini goals or poles are unavailable, I would use cones in their place.
- Pitch size and timings have been deliberately left off; this is because you will know what works best for your players.

1. Switching Play Via The Centre-Backs

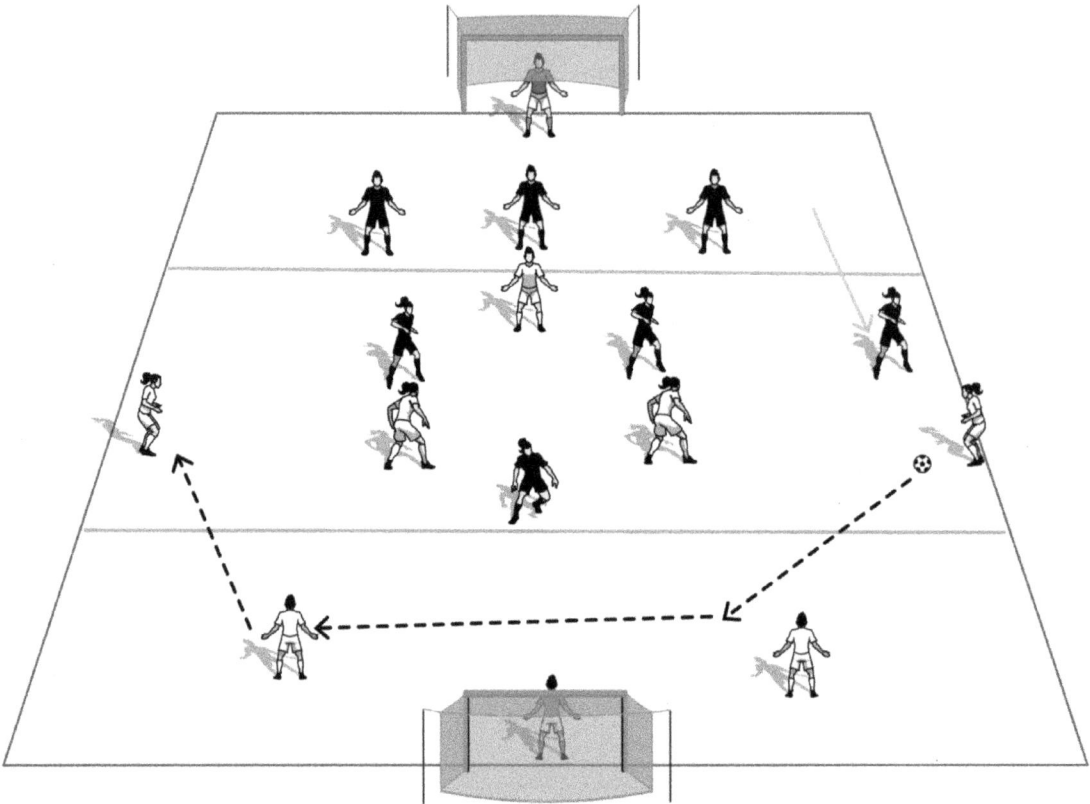

Conditions

- The team in possession has no restrictions in the final third.
- The two central defenders can drop into the first third to receive the ball unopposed.
- The out of possession team cannot press in the final third.

Progressions

- Allow one player to press in the final third to create pressure on the centre-backs.
- Allow a third defender and a second attacker to enter the defensive third.
- Continue the practice without the zonal restrictions.

Coaching Points

- Encourage the centre-backs to drop off and put space in front of them, making the back four a 'U' shape.
- Use the extra space to invite the defending team out of its shape.
- Can the possession team recognise where space has been created?
- Can midfield look to occupy this newly created space?
- Can the defending team remain compact in central areas and deny space?

2. Breaking Lines Through Central Midfield

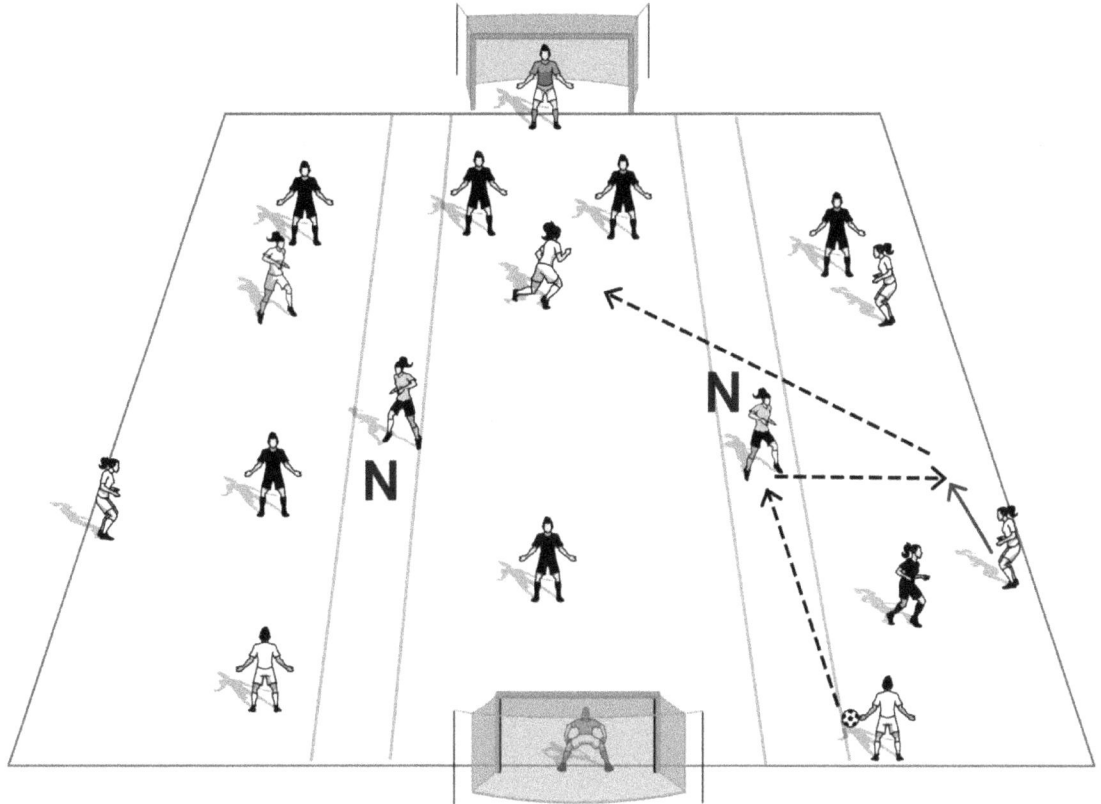

Conditions

- Play begins with the goalkeeper.
- Play comprises of five channels, including two inside channels, each containing a neutral player.
- The two neutral players are unopposed and limited to two touches.
- Players can move anywhere on the field to receive the ball.
- The aim is for the back line to break a line by building up play through the central midfield.

Progressions

- Remove the central channels; make the neutral players opposed.
- Remove the neutral players.

Coaching Points

- Can you play the safest, most direct pass possible?
- Once a line has been broken, can we get players ahead and behind the ball?
- How can we make the space as big as possible?
- Can we commit players to the attack?
- Can the defending team delay the attack?

3. Playing Away From Pressure/Playing Around The Press

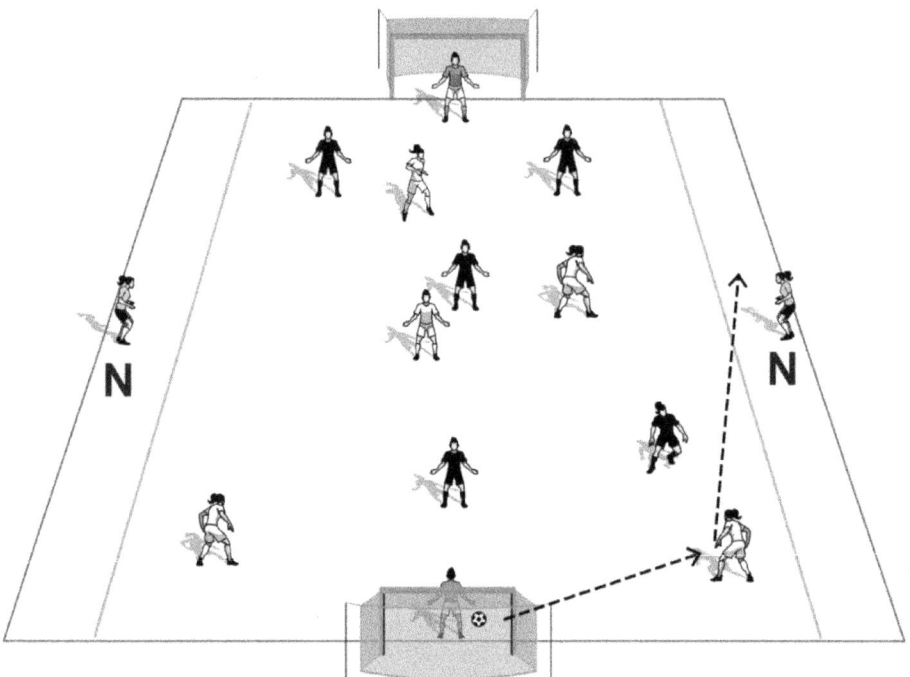

Conditions

- Play begins from the goalkeeper, who looks to play short to the centre-backs.
- There are two neutral players on each wing; they are limited to two touches.
- The centre-backs look to build up the play by using neutral players to break a line.
- The possession team gets one point for scoring a goal, two points for scoring a goal when play has gone through one neutral player, and three points when it has gone through both.

Progressions

- Force the play to go through one or both neutral players.
- Make neutral players opposed.
- Remove the neutral players.

Coaching Points

- Defenders need to balance width and depth to maximise the space.
- When neutral players are in possession, look to have passing options ahead of the ball to break a line and behind the ball to switch the play.
- Encourage decision-making processes about when to play forwards and when to play backwards.
- Can the defending team look to recover behind the ball and leave the furthest players?

4. Beating An Aggressive Press

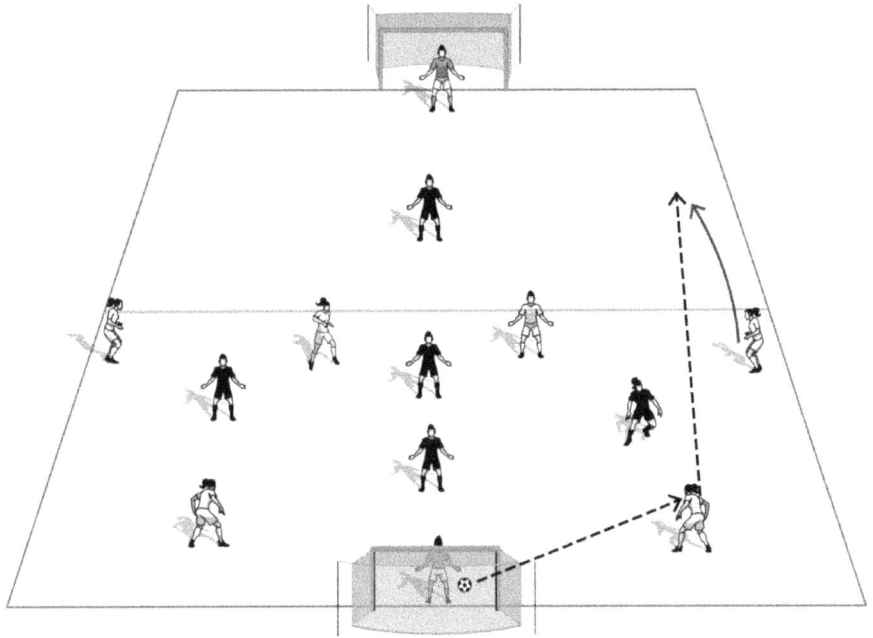

Conditions

- Play begins in the defensive half.
- The team out of possession must have only one player in the opposing half.
- The team in possession has no restrictions on where they can move.
- When the possession team is in the attacking half, the defensive team has no restrictions.

Progressions

- Increase the number of players who press.
- Decrease the size of the playing area.
- Introduce a minimum number of passes in the defensive half before attacking.

Regressions

- Reduce the number of players who can press.

Coaching Points

- Encourage the possession team to play around, through, or over the press.
- Find the balance between risk and support by making the pitch as big as possible.
- Identify the safest, most direct pass available.
- Encourage supporting runs off-the-ball.
- Can the defending team remain compact and prevent play between the lines?

5. Switching Play To Advance The Full-Back

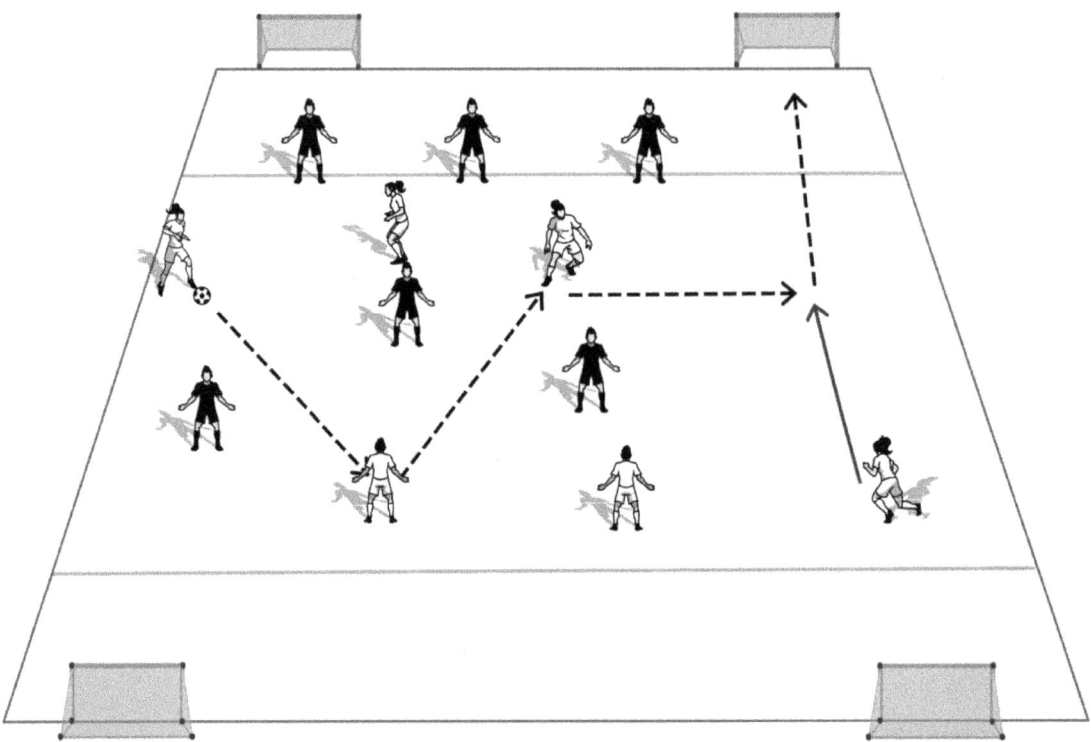

Conditions

- The possession team looks to score in one of the two mini goals.

Progressions

- The teams must switch the ball at least once before scoring.
- A player must be within one of the finishing zones before scoring.

Coaching Points

- Can we make the space as big as possible?
- Can the back line drop off to create space and allow switching?
- Encourage off-the-ball movement to occupy the space created.
- Can we invite the opposition to defend one goal before switching the angle of attack?
- Can the defending team pass players on to put pressure on the ball and leave the furthest player?

6. Advancing The Full-Backs To Break A Line

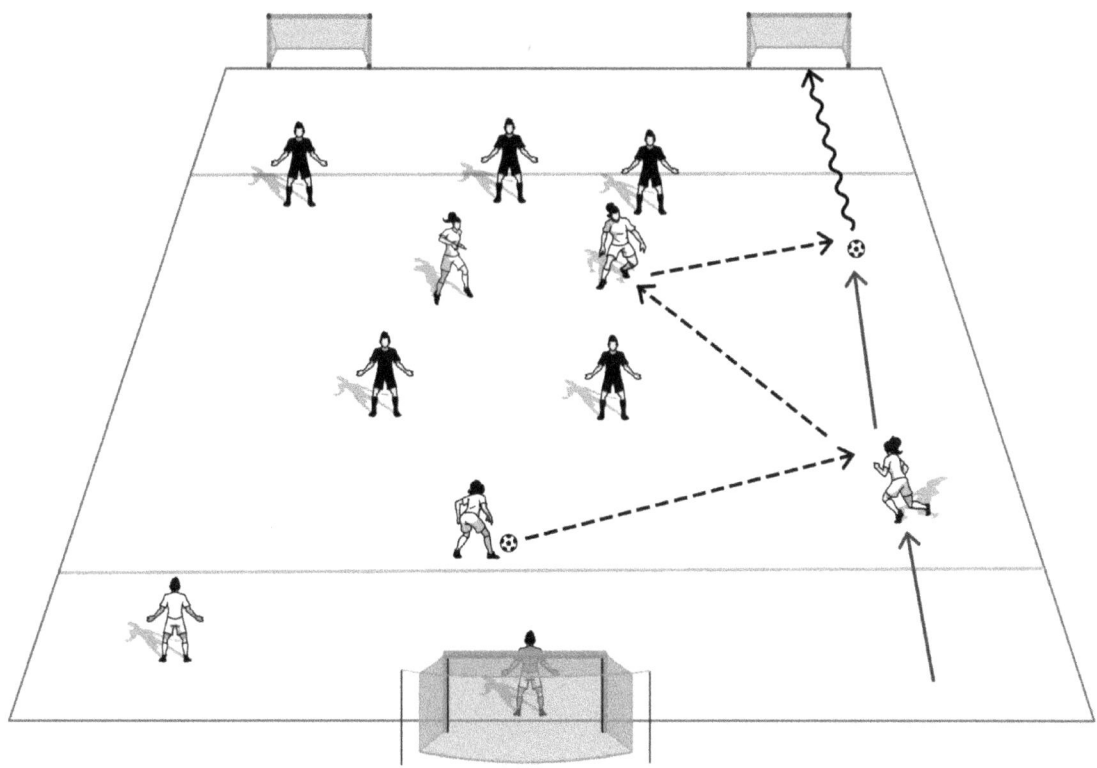

Conditions

- The white team starts in possession; one of the two full-backs can step out of the unopposed zone to join the attack. Only one full-back can step out at a time.
- The white team looks to score in one of the two mini goals.
- When the black team regains possession, they aim to score in the large central goal.

Progression

- Players can only score inside their opponent's unopposed zone.
- Only the full-backs can score in the mini goals.
- Allow both full-backs to advance when one midfielder drops into the unopposed zone.

Coaching Points

- Full-back timing to step out and offer support and provide width.
- Focus on the correct body shape to receive and play the line ball.
- Recognising when to support, when to overlap, and when to drop back into shape.

7. Playing Around The Press

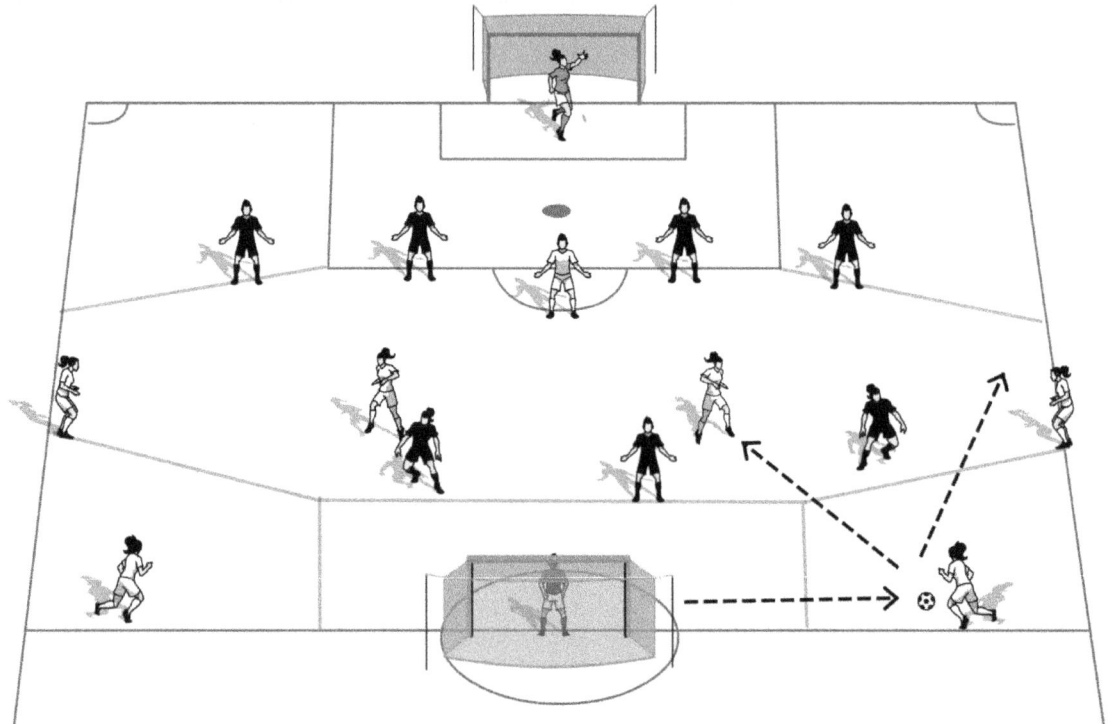

Conditions

- Play begins with the goalkeeper, who plays short to one of the centre-backs.
- The centre-back is unopposed in the corner zone of their own half.
- Each team will look to build up playing around or through the press.
- Once the centre-back has played their first pass, it becomes an open game.

Progressions

- Increase the free space to allow room for one additional defender and one attacker.
- Remove the zones and allow immediate pressure on the centre-back.
- Increase the aggression of the press by restricting players to each half.

Regression

- Force the possession team to play into the free zone first.

Coaching Points

- Look for the centre-backs to widen as much as possible.
- Full-backs to maximise height when the centre-backs are in possession to create space.
- Recognition of when to break a line with a pass.
- Midfield height to allow players to get ahead of the ball after the initial pass.
- Breaking a line with passing.

8. Denying Penetration – Four-Goal Game

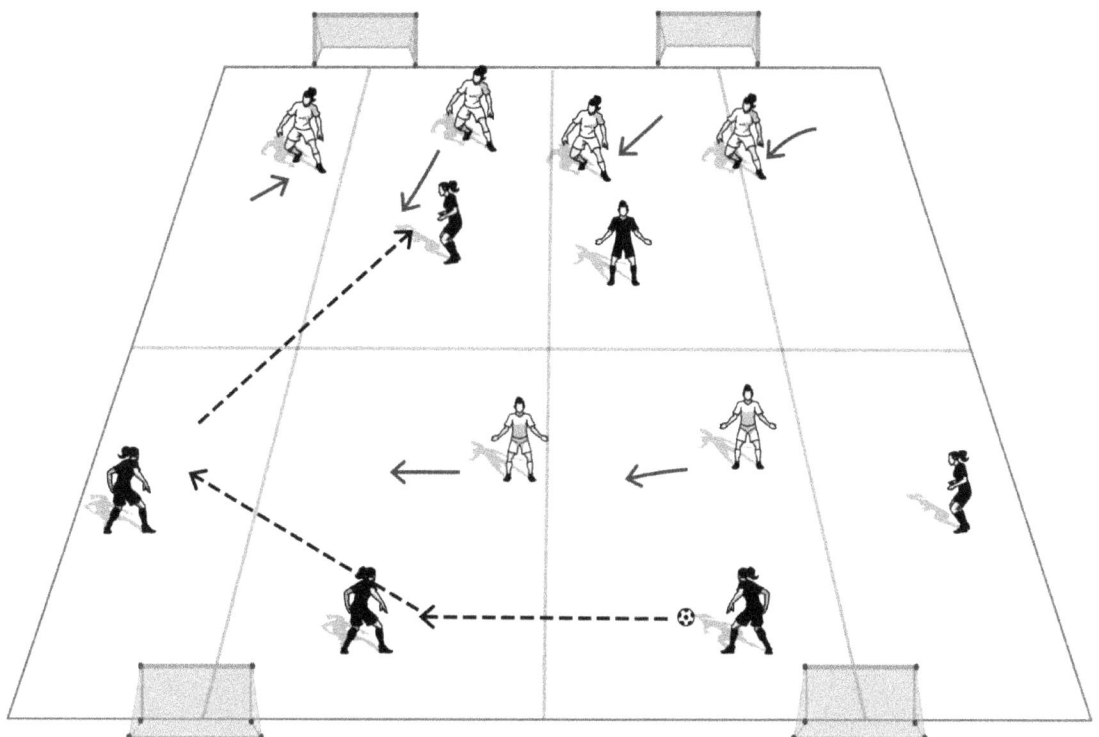

Conditions

- Each team looks to score in, and defend, two goals each.
- When in possession, the players in the defensive line must stay in their respective zones.
- Attacking players are free to move across all four attacking zones.
- The out of possession team is free to move across all the channels in their respective halves.

Progression

- The full-backs are able to move into the attacking half when in possession.
- The possession team are able to move freely within the space.

Coaching Points

- The back line to remain compact and protect the goal nearest the ball.
- Look to deny space.
- Force the opponent to turn back.
- Leave the furthest player.

9. Defending The Line – Six-Goal Game

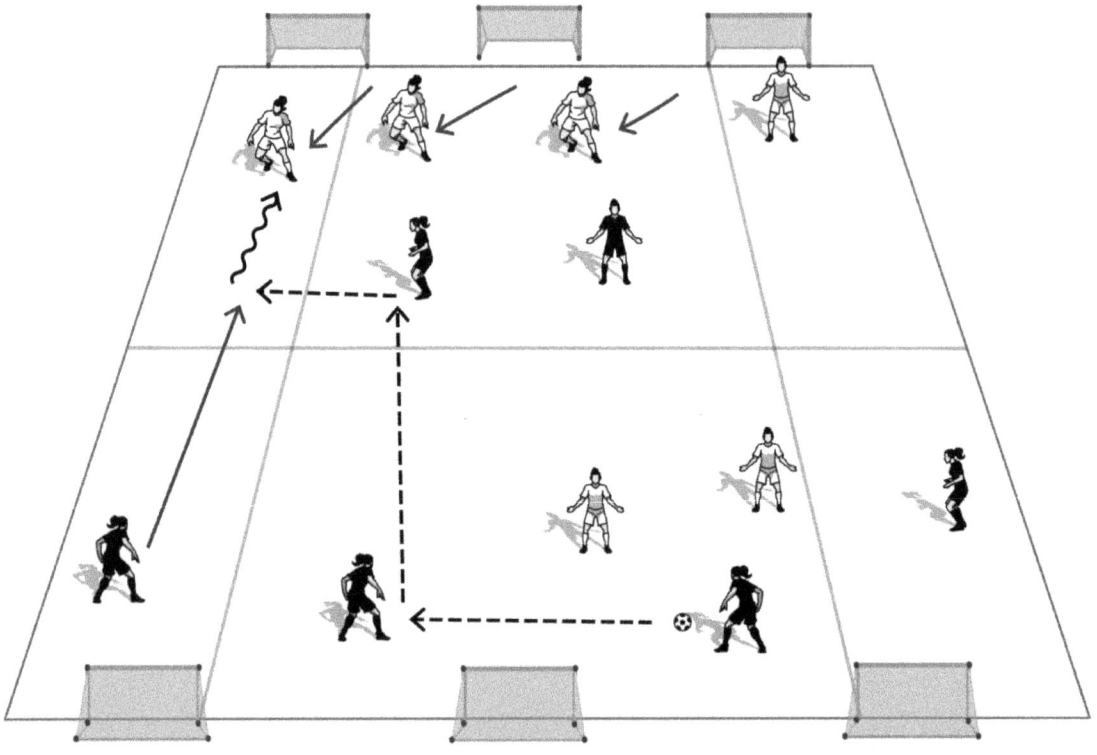

Conditions

- Each team looks to score and defend three mini goals each.
- The centre-backs are restricted to their own half.
- The full-backs have no restrictions.
- Central midfielders are restricted to the attacking half when out of possession.

Progressions

- Remove zonal restrictions for all players.

Coaching Points

- Immediate pressure on the ball.
- Protect the middle of the field.
- Stay narrow and compact.
- Protect the space behind.
- Leave the furthest player and pass players on.

10. Creating Overloads In The Build-Up Phase

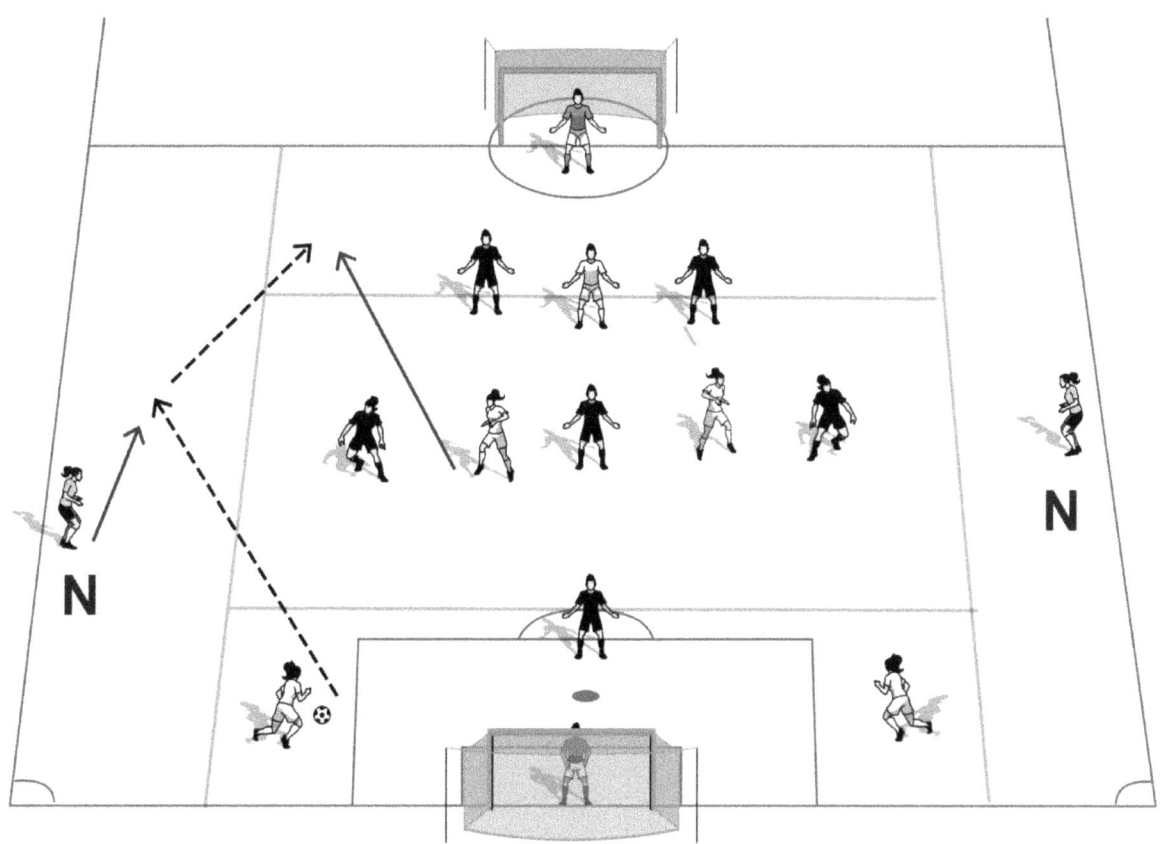

Conditions

- Play starts with the goalkeeper.
- The team in possession has two neutral players on the outside to work with.
- The neutral players are limited to two touches.
- The possession team must play out to the neutral players before they can score.

Progressions

- Make neutral players opposed.
- Remove neutral players.

Coaching Points

- Look to play the initial pass away from pressure.
- Encourage forward runs ahead of the ball to create overloads.
- Can a centre-back invite the switch of play?
- Encourage decision-making to determine the best option on the pass.
- Third-man runs in the space between the forward midfield runner and centre-back.

7. Middle Third In Possession

*"You want to win, but win in a certain way.
You want people to have a good time."*

Erik Ten Hag

For teams who look to build up through midfield, the middle third is where creativity meets stability, where attacks are initiated, and where the game is controlled. For teams who boast a strong midfield, this is the key to unlocking their full potential and penetrating the final third.

One of my favourite examples of this was the Leicester City sides of 2019/20 and 2020/21 under Brendan Rogers, who were as equally comfortable sitting deep and absorbing pressure as they were playing on the front foot, stepping into midfield and trying to get James Maddison and Harvey Barnes into the final third, or pushing full-backs Ben Chillwell, Timothy Castagne or Ricardo Pereira into attacking positions.

If their opponent was aggressive in its press, Leicester would look to play through or over the press, getting Jamie Vardy in behind early to force the opponent back. However, when the opponent adjusted to this and dropped off to deny Vardy space, they were equally capable of playing through a lower block getting Pereira and Chilwell into advanced positions in wide areas. They did this by creating space in central areas, forcing their opponent to narrow and then exploiting it by combining the movement of Maddison and Barnes with the passing of Youri Tielemans to get their full-backs into the attacking half.

Additionally, we have seen in the last 12 months how much sides value control in the midfield. Pep Guardiola and Mikel Arteta have both placed huge significance on these parts of the field by adopting a box midfield. In Guardiola's case, that has been to push John Stones or Rico Lewis alongside Rodri when they're in possession. Arteta has tried a similar approach moving Oleksandr Zinchenko inside next to Granit Xhaka allowing Leandro Trossard and Martin Odegaard to push higher up the field.

In this chapter, we explore the tactical intricacies of midfield play, delving into the importance of spatial awareness, positioning, and intelligent movement.

A quick reminder of our in possession principles:

- Make the pitch as big as we can
- Attack the space created
- Play the safest, most direct pass
- Find the free player
- Play around or through the press

Our four additional sub-principles – for playing through the midfield – are:

1. Spatial Awareness
2. Rotation in central areas
3. Maintain the ability to switch the play
4. Penetrate the final third

Make The Pitch As Big As We Can

As in Chapter 4, it is crucial that – when in possession – we continue to make the pitch as big as possible to prevent the opposition from being able to mark multiple players at once with a single marker. We want to stretch the opposition and deny them the ability to remain compact by creating as much space between our own lines as possible. The more space we occupy, the more space the defending team must cover, and they are forced into deciding which space they cover and which space they leave unoccupied.

For this reason, maintaining spatial awareness is important; as a team, we want to position ourselves strategically to create multiple passing options. This includes options both ahead and behind the ball. This allows us to break through defensive lines, both in central and wide areas, and maintain the ability to switch the ball in order to find the space in which the defence is forced to leave.

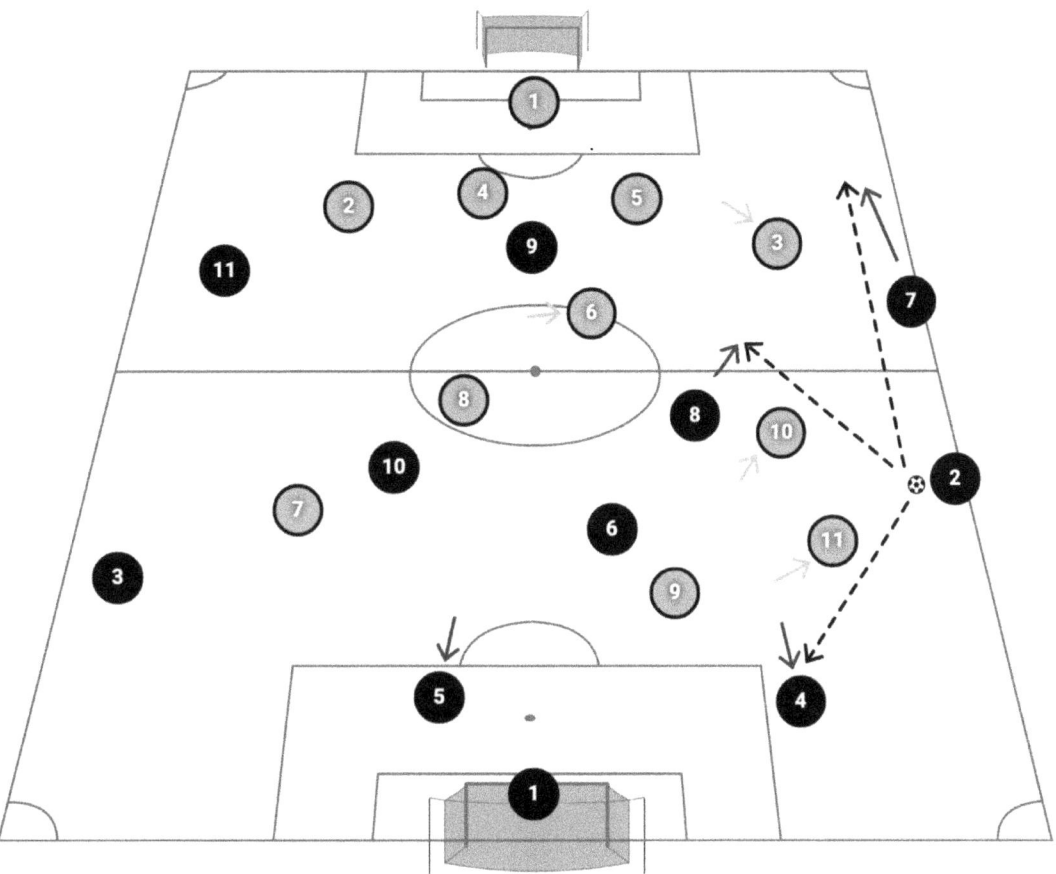

Figure 1 – Full-back in possession with multiple passing options.

In Figure 1, the right back ② is in possession with options both ahead of him to break a line ⑦ and behind him to switch the play through the centre-back ④. Because the centre-back has dropped off, it has forced the opposition left winger into a decision to either press the ball or cover the man; in turn this means the midfielder must make a decision whether or not he needs to cover the space closest to the ball. This allows our outside central midfielder ⑧ space in which to attack.

Depth is crucial in this area of the field, because if we cut off the ability to play backwards, it will allow the opponent the ability to set pressing traps and force us into areas where we are overloaded. It also makes our play incredibly predictable as the defending team can force us into safe areas away from goal.

Attack The Space Created

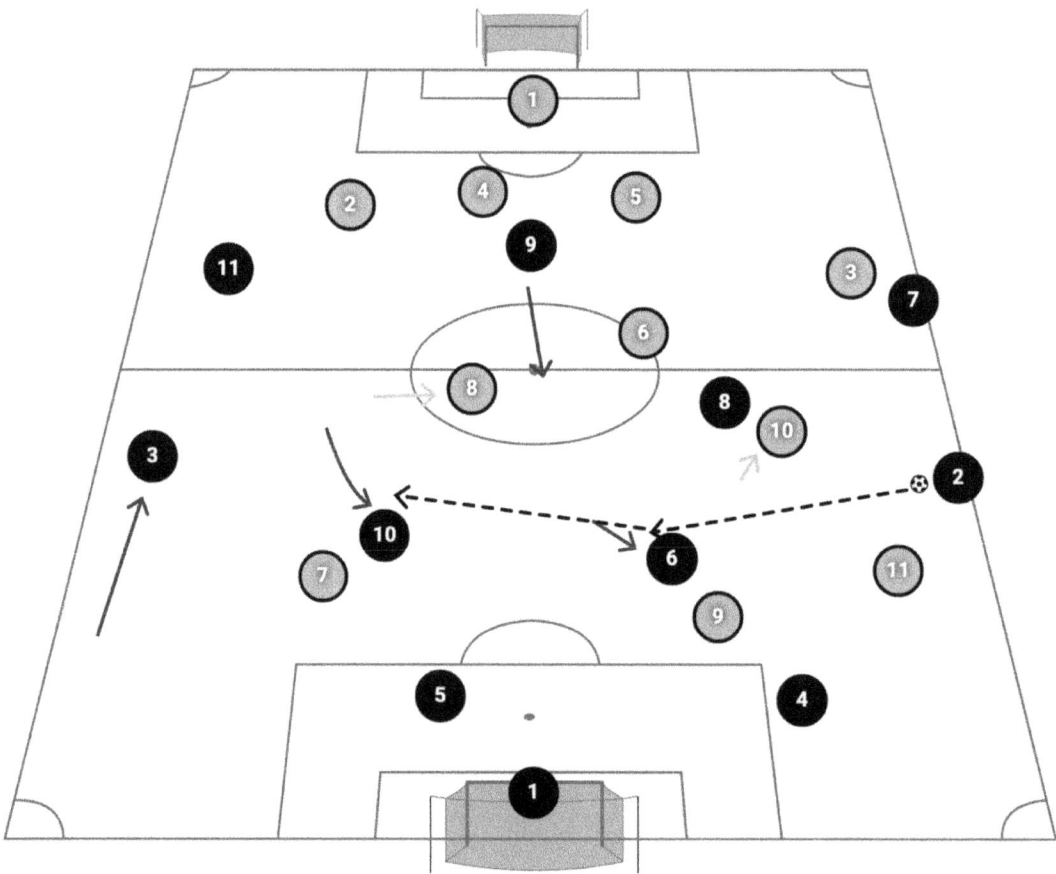

Figure 2 – Full-back in possession looking to switch the play.

When we are in midfield, we look for our midfielders to trigger movement into the space we have created with our positioning. If we've maintained multiple passing options, this allows us to get runners ahead of the ball ❽/❿ to disrupt the opposition's defensive shape and create overloads (Figure 2). If our central midfielders rotate effectively, this can create confusion and disrupt the opponent's block and force the their players into one area of the field.

Supporting players ❻ allow us to switch the play and exploit the space left vacated. Rapid positional changes ❾ make it challenging for opponents to track individual players and apply consistent pressure. This can force the opposition to adjust their defensive plans, open up spaces for our players, and create opportunities for the team to exploit.

Find The Free Player

Naturally, the opposition are going to try to create pressure on the ball carrier and deny our ability to break lines. They may do this by setting pressing traps or by creating overloads to deny us space. It's important for us that we maintain the ability to play away from that pressure and find a free player.

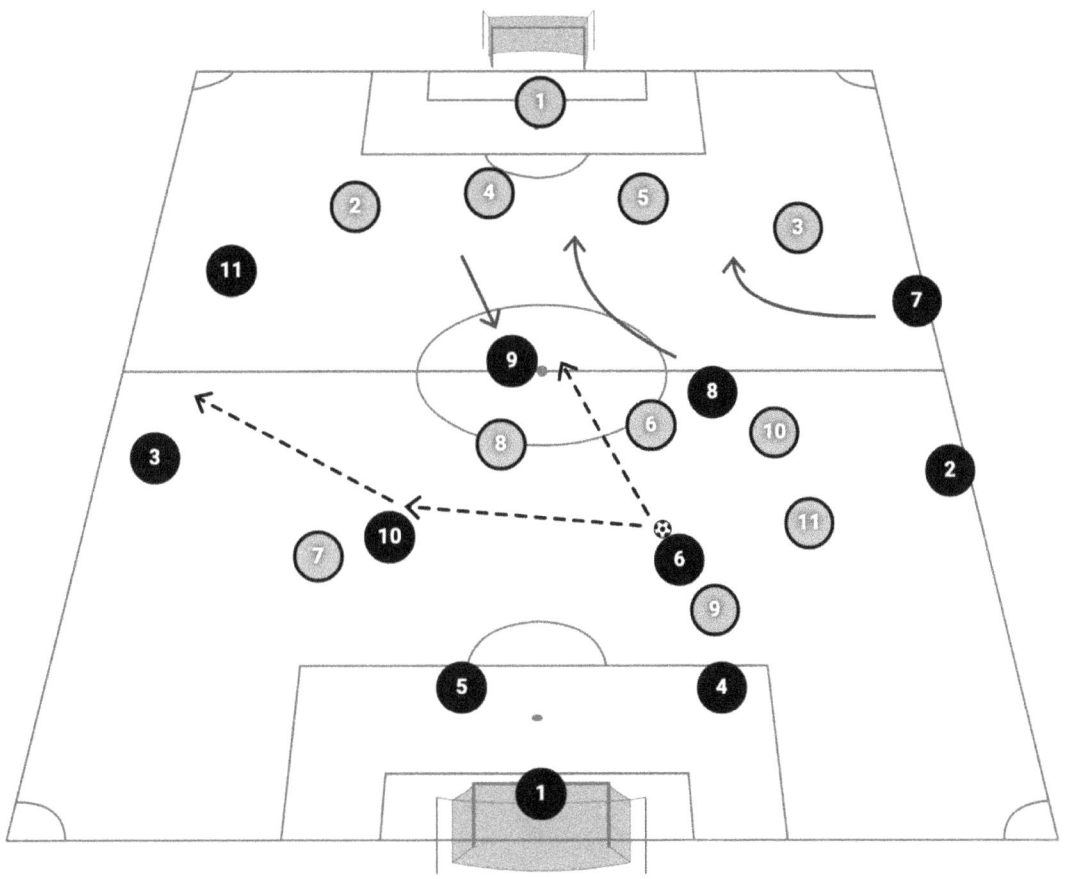

Figure 3 – Defensive Midfielder in possession with multiple passing options.

As mentioned, we want to maximise the space the opposition have to defend. We can do this by having our centre-backs to continue to drop off, maintaining a 'U' shape to prevent the opposition from narrowing their lines and denying us space to play. The centre-backs dropping off forces the opponent into making a decision: either to remain compact and allow the centre-backs space to receive the ball, or to press the centre-backs and leave the space currently occupied.

This provides us with two advantages in that if the opposition continue to drop off, the centre-backs can provide a safe out ball and the opportunity to switch the play to the opposite side of the field. If the opposition forward line look to press our centre-backs and leave the space they are defending, we can exploit the area of the field they leave and move the ball through midfield.

When switching the play to the opposite side, this allows us to bypass the opposition's block and enables us to attempt to create an overload on the opposite side. It is important that whilst we look to switch play and create overloads on the opponent's weaker side, we still look to exploit any openings in central areas (Figure 3) and break a line with a forward pass.

If they make moves to prevent the switch, this will provide space for our back line to step out with the ball and break a line into midfield. The very best creative players in the world thrive in these kinds of spaces – looking to receive the ball on the half-turn between the opposition's lines. If we're able to drag the opposition lines apart, then this creates space.

Play The Safest, Most Direct Pass

In the middle of the field, we have greater flexibility to play more direct passes as we look to penetrate the opposition's final third. However, we still want to make sure that we avoid horizontal passes or passes across our own penalty area that can be intercepted for a quick counterattack. If we lose possession with a diagonal pass, at least one player can put immediate pressure on the ball; however, if a horizontal pass is intercepted it will take both players out of the game.

At the same time, it is important that – having created the space and moved into it – we look to breach the opponent's defence by breaking lines through forward passes or dribbling. By breaking lines in the middle third, our midfield players can directly advance the ball into the attacking third.

If we are successful in combining our spatial awareness with midfield rotations, we should be able to penetrate the final third (Figure 4) and bring the attacking line into the game in areas where we can hurt the opposition.

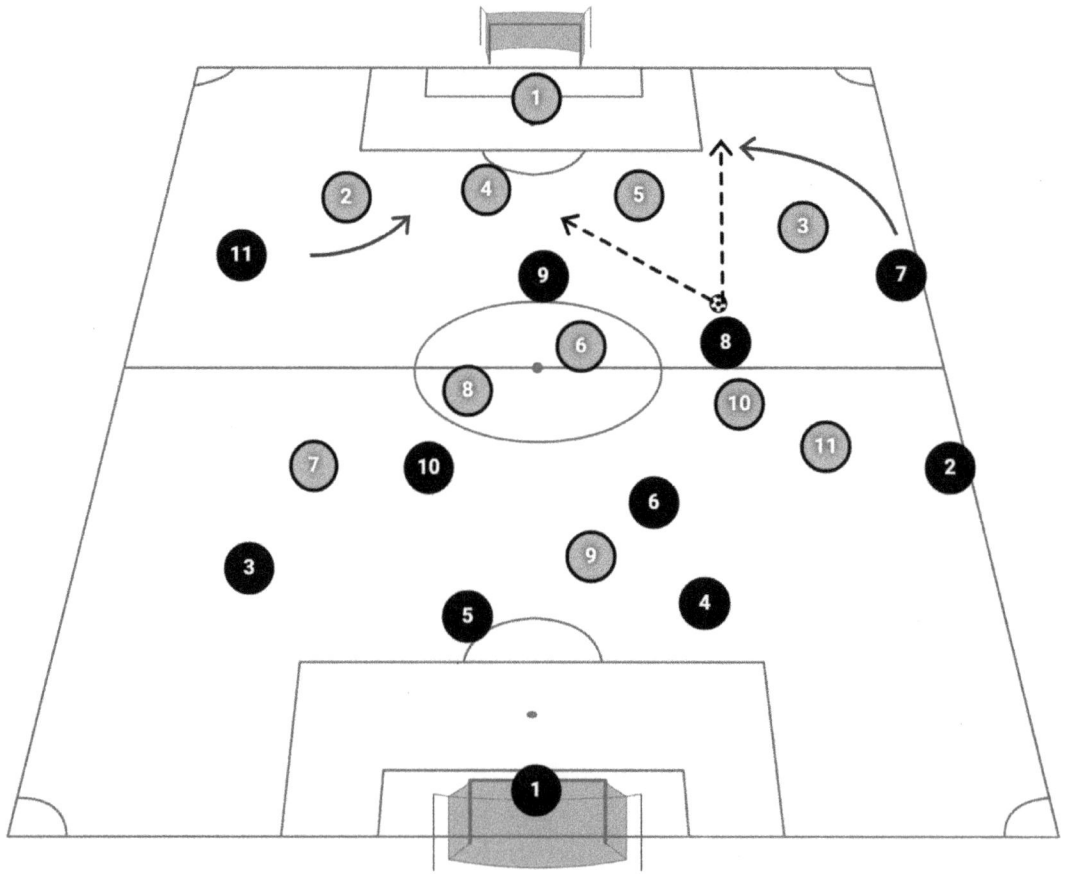

Figure 4 – Outside Midfielder in possession looking to break a line.

Conclusion

So much of a team's game can be played in the middle third, especially when the opposition invite us on as part of their defensive structure. If we maintain depth in our play, it will force the defending side into a decision about how they cover the additional space. If we can encourage our midfielders to rotate and attack this additional space, it adds unpredictability to the side's attacking play. If we combine this with an emphasis on players interchanging positions and roles, along with breaking lines into the final third, it will allow us to penetrate the opposition's defensive shape and create goalscoring opportunities.

8. Out of Possession – Middle Third

"Games are not won by those who play well,
but by those who play safe."

Diego Simeone

One cold winter Sunday afternoon, I found myself standing on the side of a windswept 3G pitch (is there any other kind?), watching two sides that my team would play in the upcoming weeks. The home side began the game with an aggressive press, looking to prevent their opponents from settling on the ball. On a small pitch, they pushed a very high line, right on the halfway line, forcing their opponents to lump it long and surrender possession. When the home side regained possession, they'd respond by doing exactly the same.

The pattern of the game was quickly established, but as the pressing players quickly tired, the pressing dropped off, even though the defensive line *continued* to push a high line. Before half-time, both teams managed to squeeze 20 players into 30 yards of space, either side of the halfway line.

As both sides were either unwilling or unable to drop their defensive line, the game dissolved into long balls over the top, with players trying to convince the referee they were still onside as they raced through to score. The final score was 5-3, but had it been a league in which assistant referees were appointed, it could have resembled a basketball game.

Whilst Pep Guardiola and Jurgen Klopp have made the high press fashionable, it's a misconception that sitting deeper and getting players organised behind the ball should be considered negative. The managers who have perfected the art of the medium block – such as Rafa Benitez, Diego Simeone or Jose Mourinho – have been branded as defensive coaches rather than coaches who have mastered ways of nullifying highly expansive attacking teams.

Back on the windswept 3G, I did not believe that both managers were uncompromising in their footballing principles. Rather, it was a result of the players' natural instincts to chase the ball in an attempt to win it back, combined with a lack of understanding of when to attack space and when to defend it.

The perception of conceding space and defending deeper can sometimes seem defeatist to players, but even the most aggressive pressing teams must sit in a lower block some of the time. It is physically challenging (nay impossible) to maintain a high press for every minute of every game. Even the most aggressive teams use a medium block to get into a resting press and defend the space whilst conserving their energy.

There are times when sitting in a medium block will have its tactical advantages for an aggressive pressing team, as the better teams will look to invite an aggressive press and exploit any gaps left by that team's aggression. Sitting in a medium block has many more benefits, including forcing the opposition into safe areas and delaying their attacks by cutting off certain areas of the field.

Forcing the possession team to play more sideways and backwards passes – as the space they look to play into is occupied by defenders – allows the defending team to set pressing traps to win the ball back in good areas of the pitch where they possess an overload.

Additionally, defending deeper allows the defending team to engage high enough up the field to prevent the opponent from creating a goalscoring opportunity and getting the ball in behind the defence. It forces them high enough to leave space in behind their defence for a quick counterattack.

Here is a reminder of our key defending principles:

- Remain as compact as possible
- Leave the furthest player
- Protect the middle of the field
- Let the opposition play in safe areas
- Make the opposition's play predictable

In this chapter, we look to add the following sub-principles:

1. Prevent the opponent from receiving the ball between the lines
2. Force the opponent to play sideways or backwards
3. Occupy the space between the midfield and defensive units
4. Track runners looking to get in behind or making blind side runs

Remain As Compact As Possible

It's crucial that – when we are defending in the middle of the field – we remain a compact unit and look to deny the opposition space to play between our defensive lines. In the previous chapter, we covered trying to make the space as big as possible to encourage midfield rotation between defensive lines.

It stands to reason that the opposition will look to do the same to us when we are out of possession. If we allow a player to drop between the lines unopposed, that will provide that player with time to turn or potentially hit a second direct pass through our press and start a threatening attack in behind our defence. In this instance, it's critical that your midfield can either close the space ahead of them or drop into the space behind them as a unit (Figure 1).

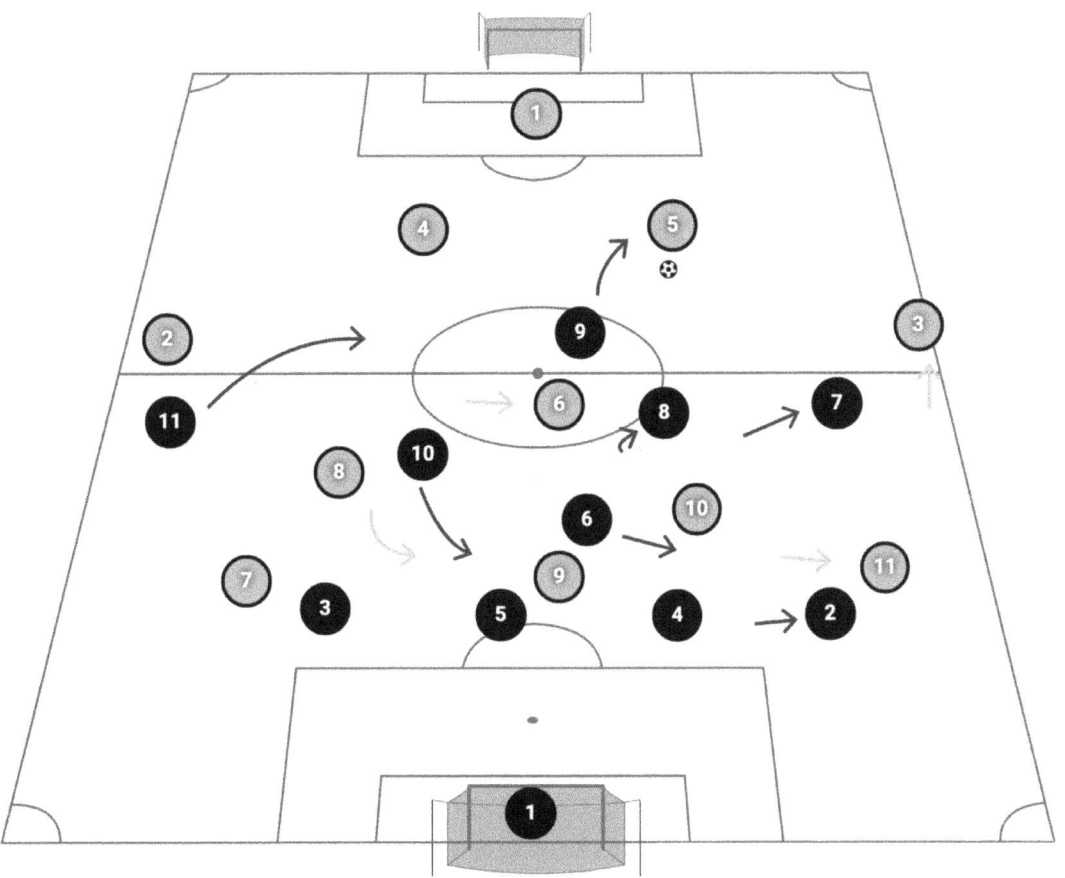

Figure 1 – Defending with a balanced shape.

It is important that our defensive units look to remain as compact and as close to each other as possible, to prevent the opposition from freely occupying space in between them. If one defensive line is too far or too close to another, it will allow the opponent to create overloads in the space. If we deny them space between our lines, it will prevent them from attacking quickly.

Leave The Furthest Player

In addition to leaving no space between the lines, we want to remain as compact as possible within our lines. When the ball is in central areas (Figure 1), we want to make sure we leave no space on either side of our centre-backs ❺ / ❹ by having our full-backs ❸ / ❷ narrow to prevent the forwards from getting into the half-space. When our defensive formation remains compact, it makes it difficult for the opponent to find passing lanes and exploit spaces between defenders.

The team in possession will look to stretch the pitch and make us cover as much ground as possible. This means we must cover the players closest to the ball, passing on players furthest from the ball who pose less of an immediate threat to our goal. If we remain compact and prevent switches of play, we can isolate players on the far side of the field without the need to man-mark.

If the side in possession looks to try and find these players with a long ball, the defensive unit can either look to put pressure on the ball to prevent the switch or have enough time to see it coming and adjust their defensive positioning.

Protect The Middle Of The Field

Sometimes, we have to accept that the opposition are going to have the ball in good areas, are going to do good things with it, and we won't be in a position to regain possession. In these situations, we may have to accept that they have possession, but we can *still* dictate where we want them to have it.

If the opposition look to stretch us with runs ahead of the ball, or in behind, it may be with the aim of trying to drag defensive players out of shape to create overloads in the vacated space. It is vital that defensive units remain disciplined, passing runners on and protecting the middle of the field – thus narrowing the angle of attack for the team in possession. The very best teams will look to try and pull the midfield out of central areas to leave the defence exposed to deep runs.

We can look to prevent this by making sure that we always have a player protecting the back four. Former Manchester United coach Rene Meulensteen used to talk about the area in front of the back four where, if one player left to put pressure on the ball, then another player must drop in to occupy that space. This prevents the back line from being overloaded by third-man runs from the opponent's midfield lines (Figure 2).

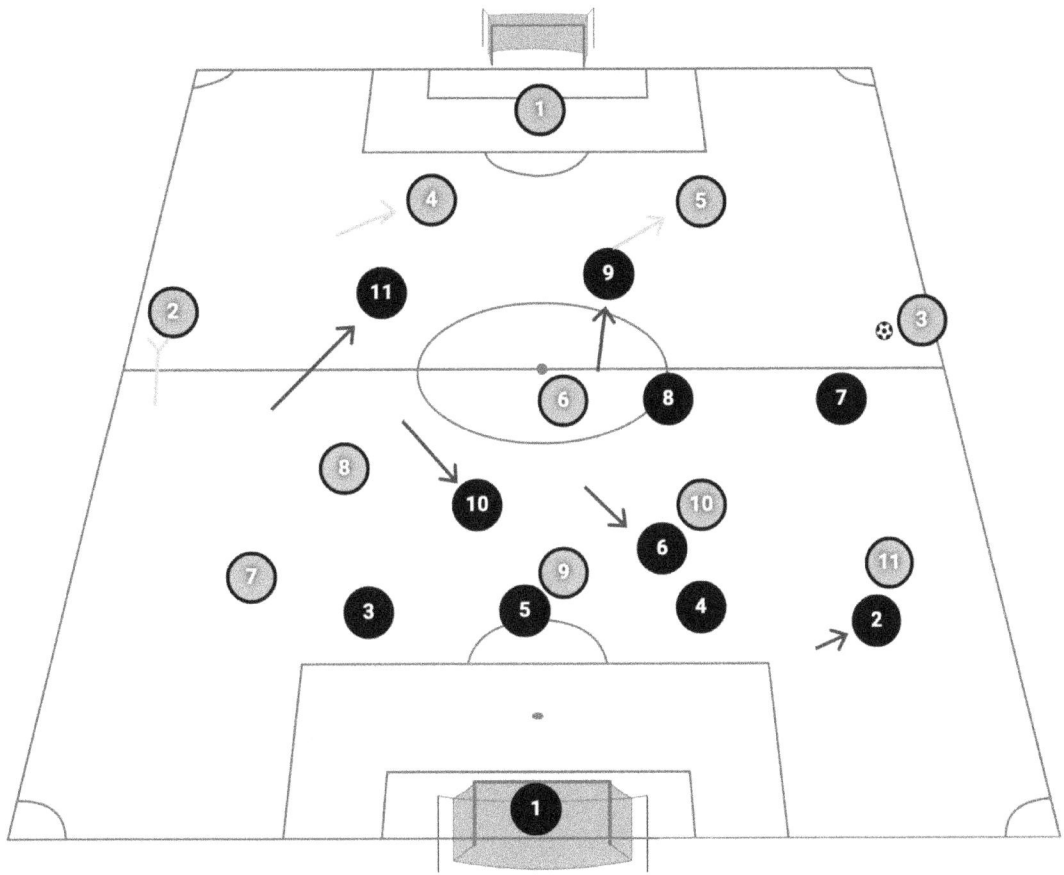

Figure 2 – Looking to force the play into central areas.

If the right-sided centre midfield ❽ is pulled out wide to protect a passing lane, the holding midfielder ❻ will look to slide across as protection. In this instance, we're looking for the far-side central midfielder ❿ to tuck into the central position to act as cover for the pivot and prevent our opponent from getting success with blind-side runs.

Let The Opposition Play In Safe Areas

A key characteristic of playing in a deeper block is that it requires players to have greater defensive awareness and discipline. It is crucial that players understand *when* to put pressure on the ball or *when* to defend the space that they occupy.

If an attacking unit is too aggressive in its press, then it will leave space behind it for the opponent to exploit. Good possession teams will actively look to do this by inviting teams to press by sitting deep and then looking to play in the space they immediately leave, with midfielders dropping in to receive the ball.

They're looking to take advantage of aggressive forwards looking to leave the shape and press in isolation, thus leaving a huge gap between their attacking and midfield lines. It's important for us to have the discipline to prevent the opposition playing through, and delay the speed of their attack.

We look to do this by conceding spaces which we cannot press, by occupying forward passing lines, and remaining as compact as possible. In Figure 2, the winger **7** is looking to block the full-back's passing option and force their opponent backwards. The forward **9** is, in turn, moving across to prevent the centre-back from making a forward pass.

In remaining compact and not conceding the space, we allow the opposition to play in their own third, thus preventing them from playing into space ahead of them and nullifying their attack far from our penalty area.

Make The Opposition's Play Predictable

If we're sat in a compact shape with 11 players behind the ball (positioned between the ball and our penalty area), this makes it difficult for our opponents to break us down. If we allow the opponent to play backwards and/or sideways passes across their own defensive line, it makes their patterns of play predictable.

Less space for the opposition to play provides us with an opportunity to delay the opposition and nullify their attack by cutting off forward passing lanes. However, we still want to win the ball back at some stage! Allowing the opponent to play in certain areas means we will have additional players in deeper areas when they try to break lines so – as the ball goes backwards – we aim to push up as a unit (Figure 3).

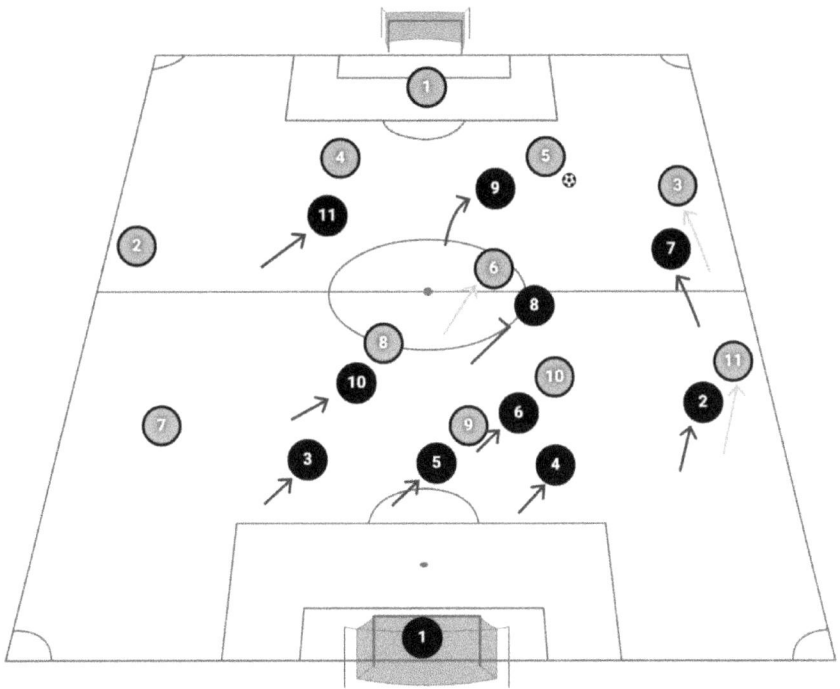

Figure 3 – Preventing the switch and setting a pressing trap.

This allows us to set pressing traps in good areas to try to regain the ball and launch quick counterattacks. We can do this by cutting off certain areas of the field and trying to prevent the switch, forcing the opposition to play the ball forwards, where we are happy for them to do so (Figure 4).

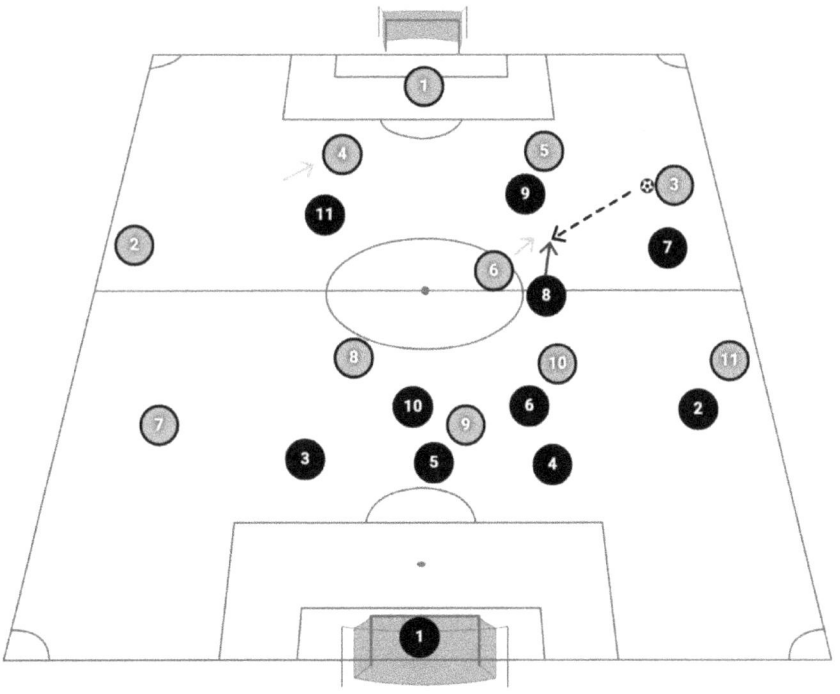

Figure 4 – Triggering the pressing trap.

Conclusion

There are certain realities that we face as coaches. Unless we're able to train every single day, we are more likely to be forced into utilising deeper blocks, regardless of our desired footballing principles. It's equally likely that players will need to be coached when *not* to press and defend the space; instinct will take over, and players will go chasing the ball all over the field.

One of the crucial aspects of setting up our players in a medium block is to convey the message that *we are not being negative* or *less ambitious*. Instead, we need to reinforce how this approach lessens physical demands on players, provides us with greater tactical flexibility, and adds greater defensive security. Crucially, it also allows us to set terms on which we aim to regain possession!

9. Middle Third Practices

In this chapter, we look at the practices for the middle third of the pitch, both in and out of possession. Each of these practices has been designed so that the coach can focus on the middle third of the field. As in Chapter 6, the coaching points differ, with some focused on in possession, some out of possession and some with both. These points aim to provide guidance and demonstrate how they are linked with the previous chapters. These coaching points can be amended based on how the coach sees fit, in terms of their aims and the needs of the players. The same practice can have many different coaching points based on *your* needs.

Key

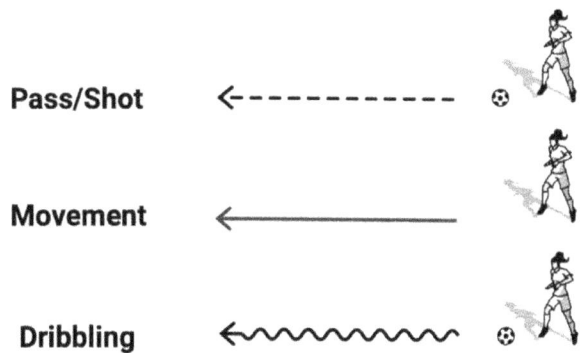

Reminders

- Throughout these practices, where I have included goalkeepers, this is to demonstrate how they can be used in the practice. If there are no goalkeepers, then they can be substituted for a mini goal or gate with a condition such as a 'two touch finish'.
- I have used the same number of players throughout the practices for uniformity, but have designed them so they can be adjusted for 8-18 players. If you are working with an odd number of players, working with a neutral player or 'magic player' should not impact the realism of the practice too greatly.
- Where I have used multiple goals or poles, this is to demonstrate the target that players are aiming to play to or through. Where mini goals or poles are unavailable, I would use cones in their place.
- Pitch size and timings have been deliberately left off; this is because you will know what works best for your players.

1. Midfield Rotations In Central Area

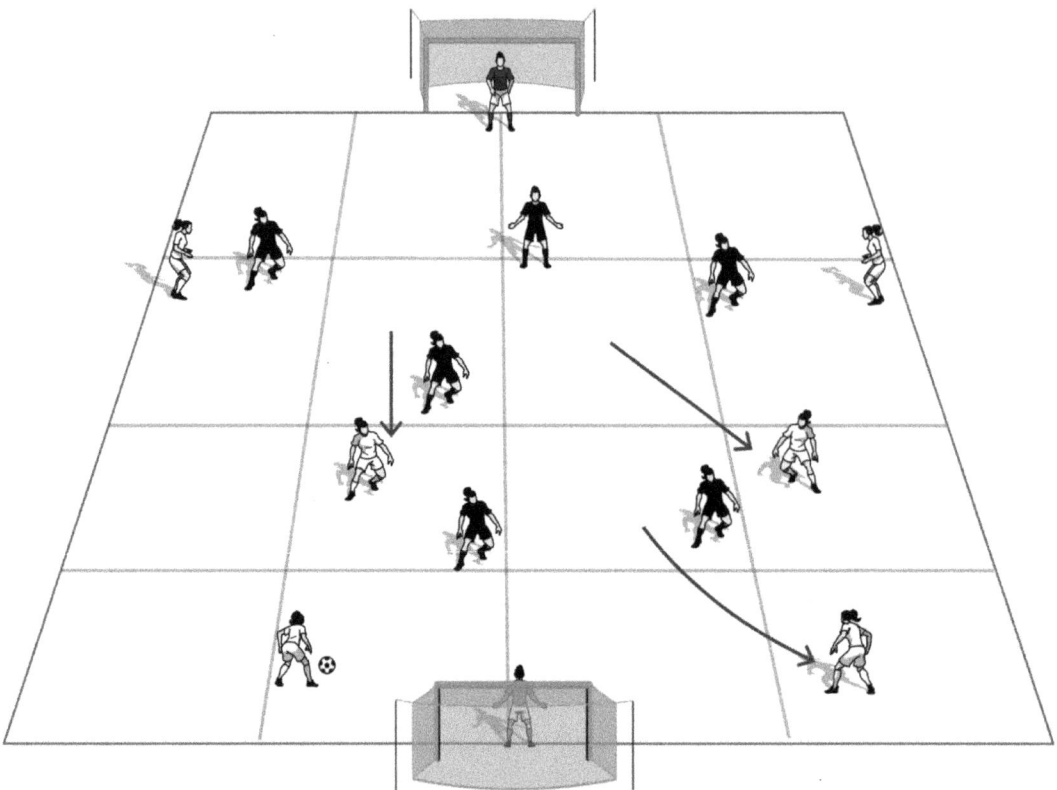

Conditions

- A goal can be scored at any time. The possession team is restricted to one player per zone.
- The possession team can move into unoccupied zones or swap occupied zones.
- The team out of possession are free to move anywhere.

Progressions

- Restrict certain players to specific zones to challenge body shape and movement.
- Remove zones and encourage the same rotations.

In Possession Coaching Points

- Correct body shape to link passes.
- Encourage movement around and away from the ball.
- Avoid horizontal passes.

Out of Possession Coaching Points

- Remain compact.
- Defend the centre of the field.
- Force away from the goal.

2. Penetrating The Final Third Through The Half Space

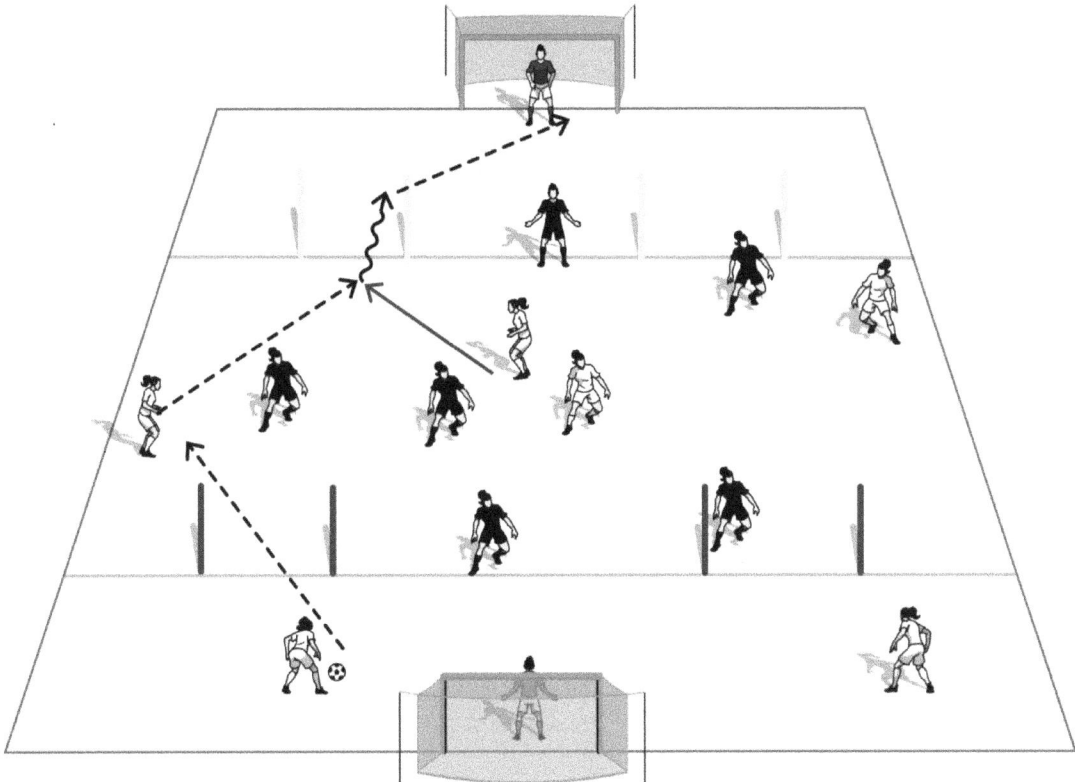

Conditions

- Play starts in the middle zone.
- The team in possession looks to dribble or play a pass through the gate in the half-space before creating a goalscoring opportunity.
- If the team out of possession wins the ball higher than the gates, they can attempt to score without going through the gates.

Regression

- Make it a non-directional game and reward teams for playing through as many gates as possible.

Progression

- Increase the number of players in the central zone to decrease the space to play.

Coaching Points

- Encourage movement ahead of the ball to stretch the play.
- Can we break a line with a pass?
- Can we receive on the half turn to continue forward momentum?

3. Playing Between The Lines To Attack In Central Areas

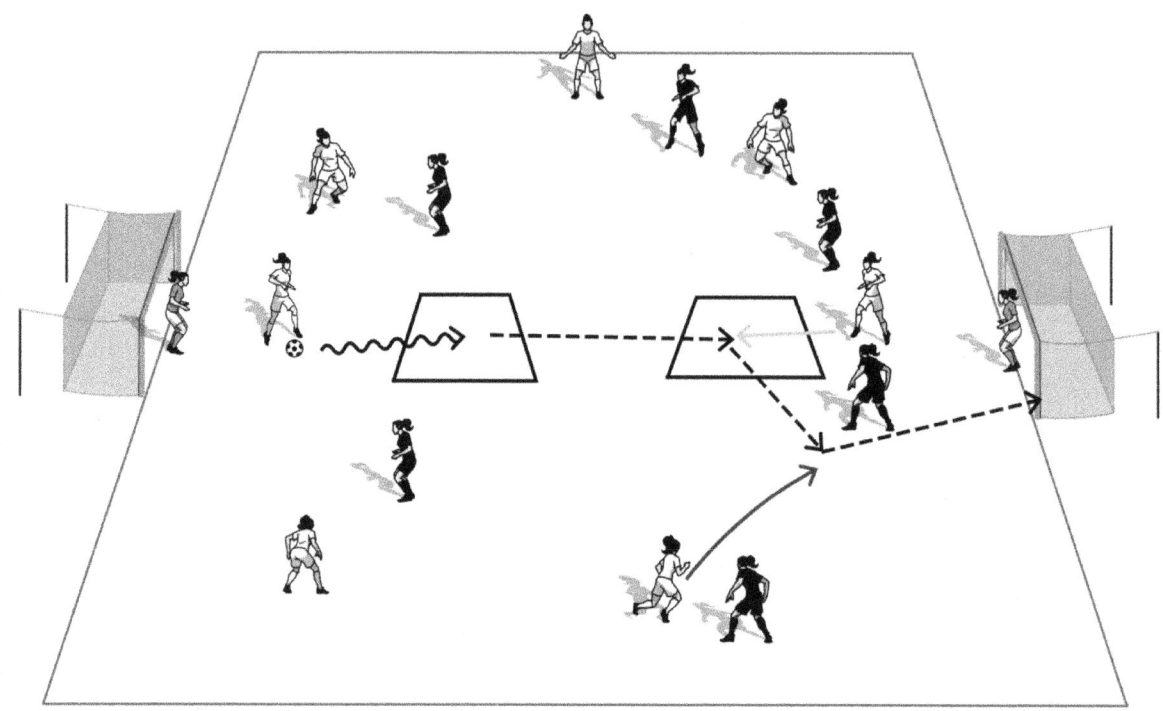

Conditions

- Play starts with the goalkeeper, and players are not restricted to where they can play.
- There are two free zones located centrally, which can be dribbled into unopposed, or where players can drop in to receive the ball.
- Players cannot stand in these areas and must time their runs to receive passes.

Progression

- Allow defensive players to follow attacking players into the free zone to create 1v1s.
- Remove the free zones and encourage players to continue the theme of the session.

Coaching Points

- Encourage defensive players to break lines and step out with the ball.
- Encourage attacking players to drop in between the lines to receive.
- Create passing options once a player has moved into the free zone.
- Encourage vertical movement outside any free zone.

4. Breaking Lines in Wide Areas

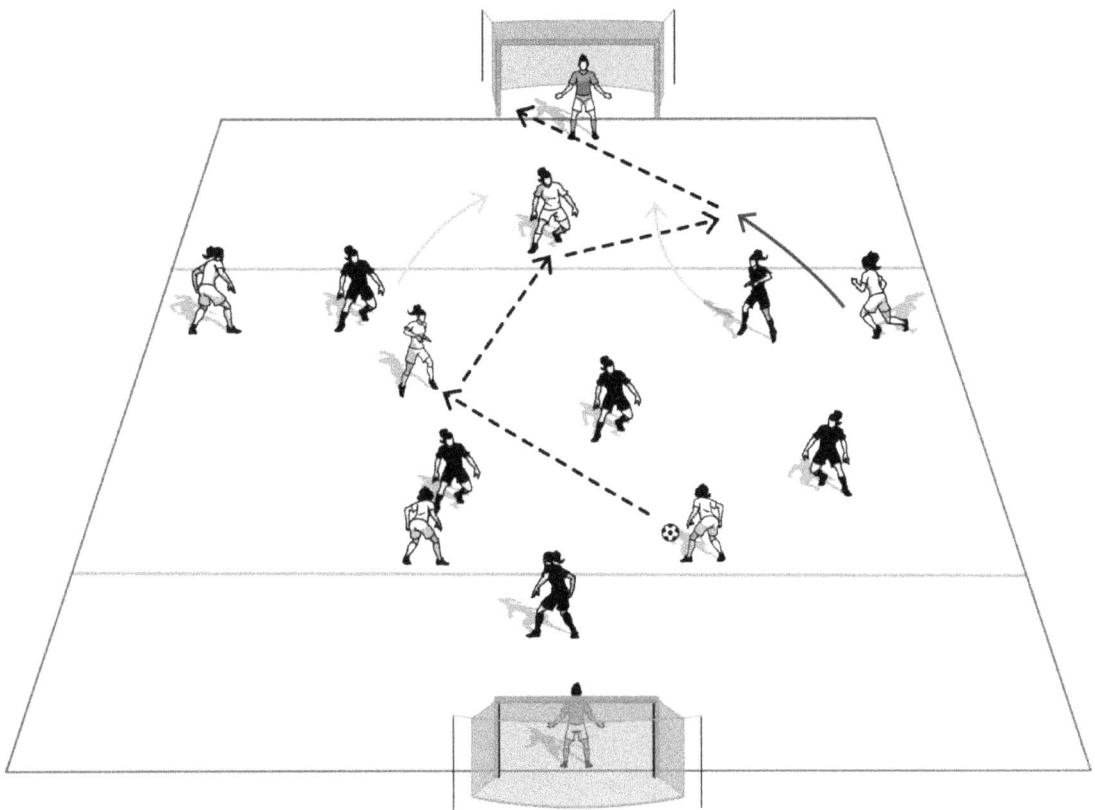

Conditions

- Players start in the middle zone with the exception of the centre forwards and goalkeepers.
- Play always begins in the middle zone.
- The possession team looks to break a line into the final third by either playing into the centre forward or by the wingers running onto a through ball.
- Two attackers can join the centre forward in the attack, whilst two defenders can drop into the defensive zone.

Coaching Points

- Triggers to start the attack.
- Through balls in front of the wide players.
- Third man runs off the ball.
- Stretch the play.

Progression

- Increase the number of attackers and defenders allowed into the end zone.

5. Switching Play Through Midfield

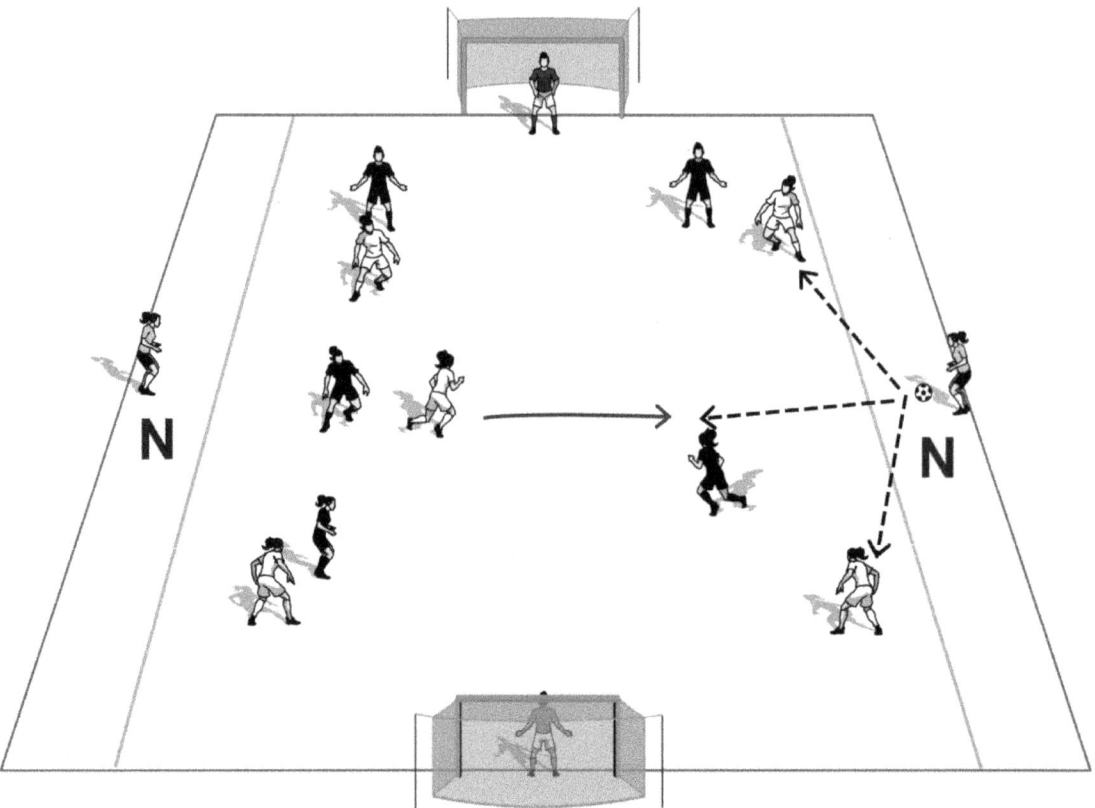

Conditions

- Play starts with the keeper and two neutral players on the outside.
- Neutral players are on a two-touch limit and are unopposed.
- Possession must be switched to the two neutral players before a goal can be scored.

Progressions

- Neutral players are limited to one touch.
- One point for a normal goal, two points when one neutral is involved in the build-up, three points when both neutral players are involved in the build-up.
- Remove unopposed neutrals.

Coaching points

- Players ahead of, and behind, the neutral player are used to stretch the opposition.
- Movement into the space is created.
- Midfield rotation.
- Dropping off to receive.

6. Midfield Rotation And Third-Man Runs Into The Final Third

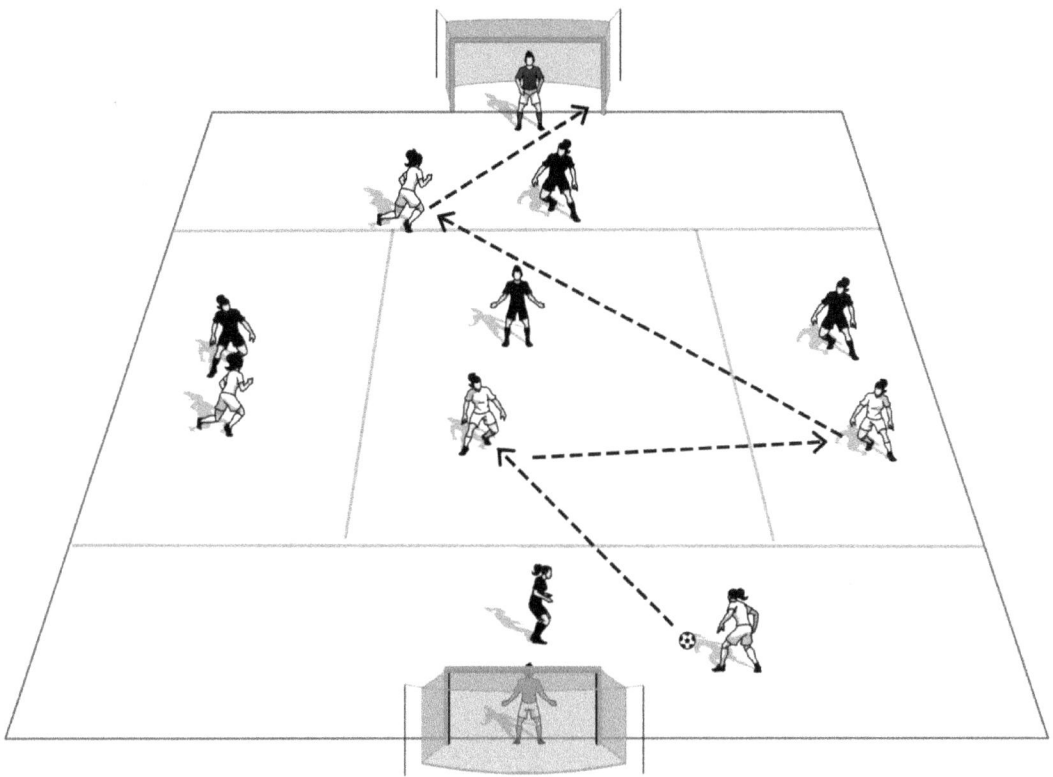

Conditions

- Play starts from a central defender who is unopposed (the forward is passive).
- The defender plays into the central area to one of three central midfielders.
- The three midfielders are restricted to their zones and must combine to play through, and into, the striker in the final third.
- A midfielder joins the attack to create a 2v1 overload in the attacking third.

Progressions

- Allow centre midfielders to swap zones.
- Remove the channels in the middle third.
- Allow two attackers and one defender into the final third to create a 3v2.
- Remove all zones to have an open game. Encourage the breaking of lines.

Coaching Points

- Midfield rotation to create and exploit space.
- Open body shapes to receive the ball.
- Third-man runs.
- Direct Play.

7. Advancing The Full-Back, Six-Goal Game

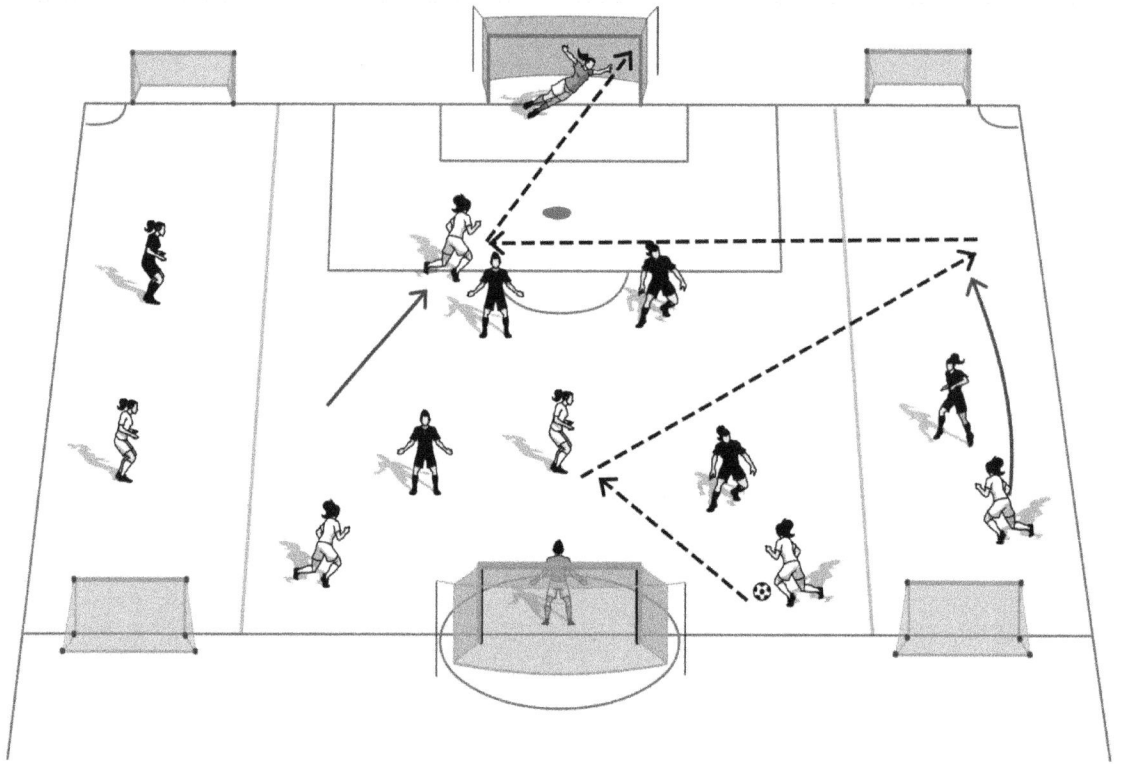

Conditions

- Each team defends and attacks three goals.
- Wide players are restricted to the wide areas and are 1v1.
- The team in possession will receive one point for a wide player scoring in the wide mini goal.
- The team in possession will receive three points for scoring in the central goal.

Progressions

- Award an extra point if a central goal is scored using an outside player in the build-up.
- Remove the zonal restrictions.

Regression

- Make the outside players unopposed.

Coaching Points

- The positioning of wide players to receive the ball on the outside.
- The positioning of wide players to take on their opponent 1v1.
- The positioning of players ahead of the ball to stretch the attack.

8. Defending The Overload In Central Areas

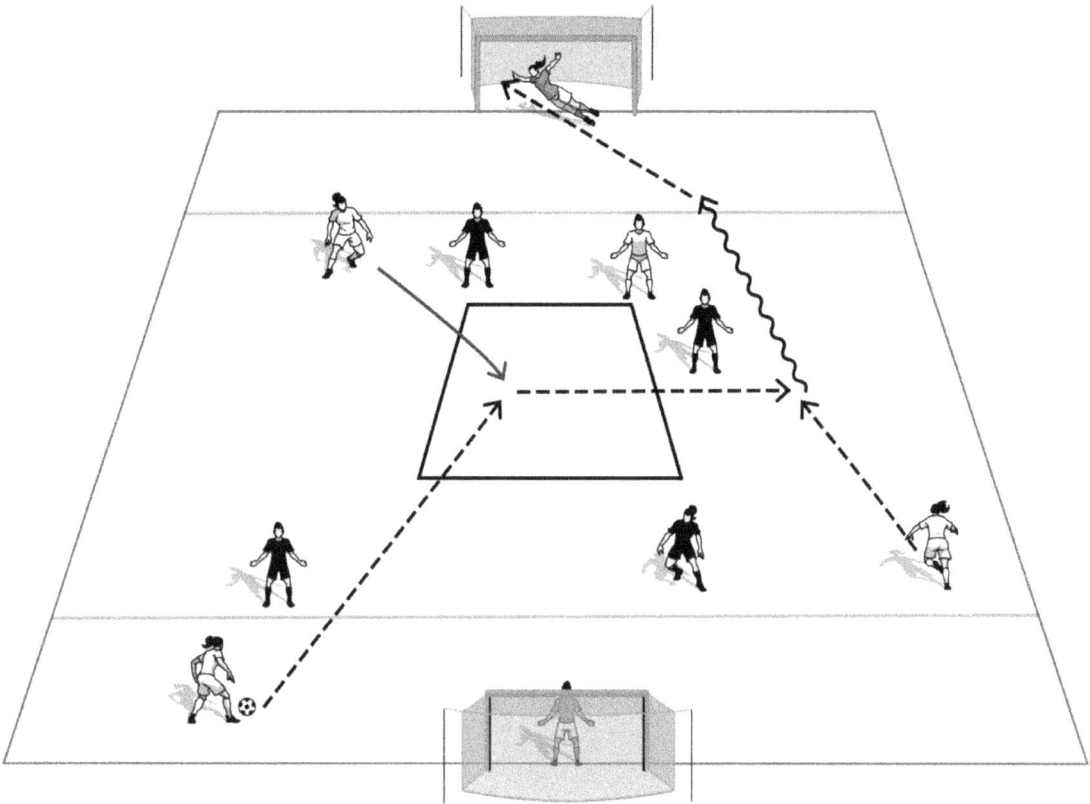

Conditions

- The team in possession looks to play through a neutral player to score.
- The team out of possession must defend the central space.
- When an out of possession team wins the ball back, they look to score immediately.

Progressions

- Make this a directional game where the team in possession must play through the central area to score.
- Remove the neutral player from the central area and encourage midfield rotation into the central zone.

Coaching Points

- Close the space between the players.
- Force the play away from central areas.
- Get between the ball and the target player.
- Pass players on.
- Leave the furthest players.

9. Playing Away From Pressure To Stretch The Play

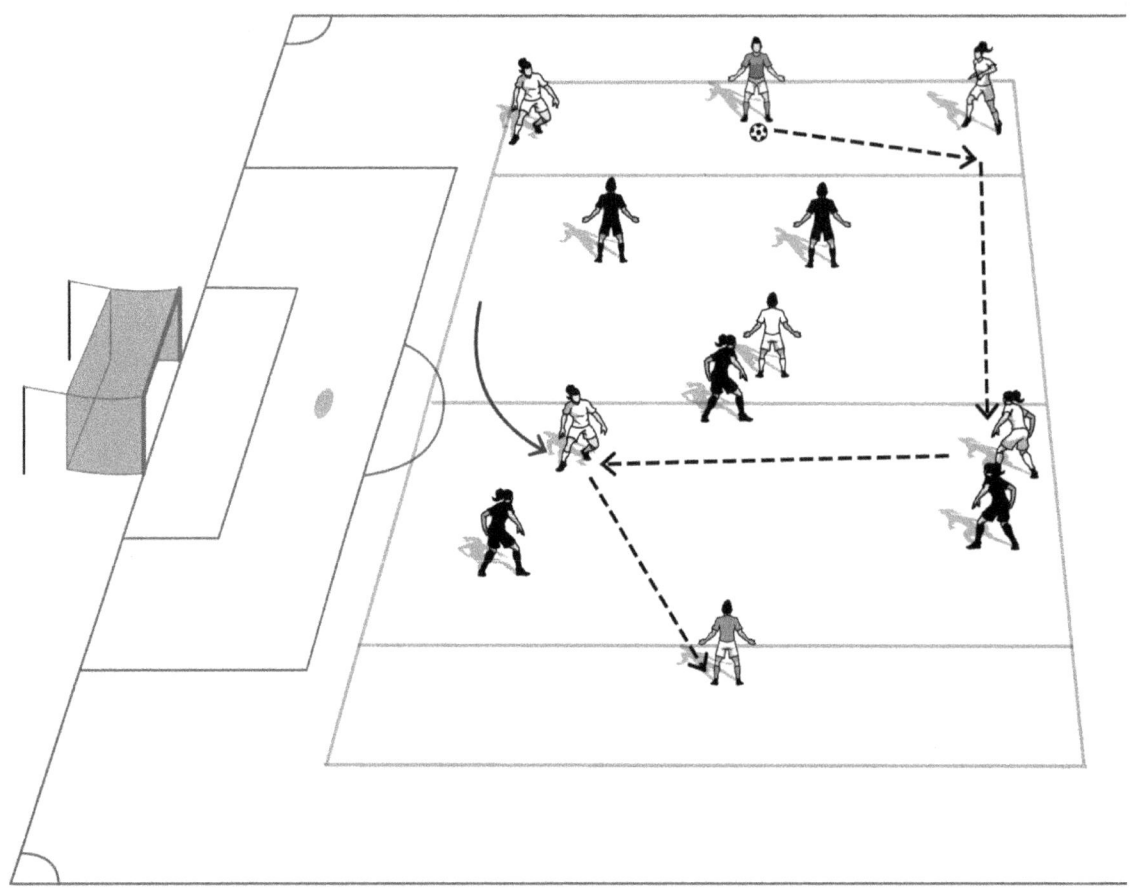

Conditions

- The possession team looks to move the ball from each end zone to the goalkeepers.
- When a team intercepts the ball, they must switch play to the opposite half.
- When the goalkeeper receives the ball, two players must drop into the end zone to receive the ball.
- Defenders can play around or through the goalkeeper to build into midfield.

Progressions

- Restrict players to specific zones to increase the challenge to rotate.
- Players can only pass into the keeper from either end zone.

Coaching Points

- The aim is to encourage players to take up unnatural positions to stretch the play.
- Encourage rotation into space created by stretching the play.
- Encourage playing into a central player under pressure so they can play a pass away from pressure.

10. Eight-Goal Game

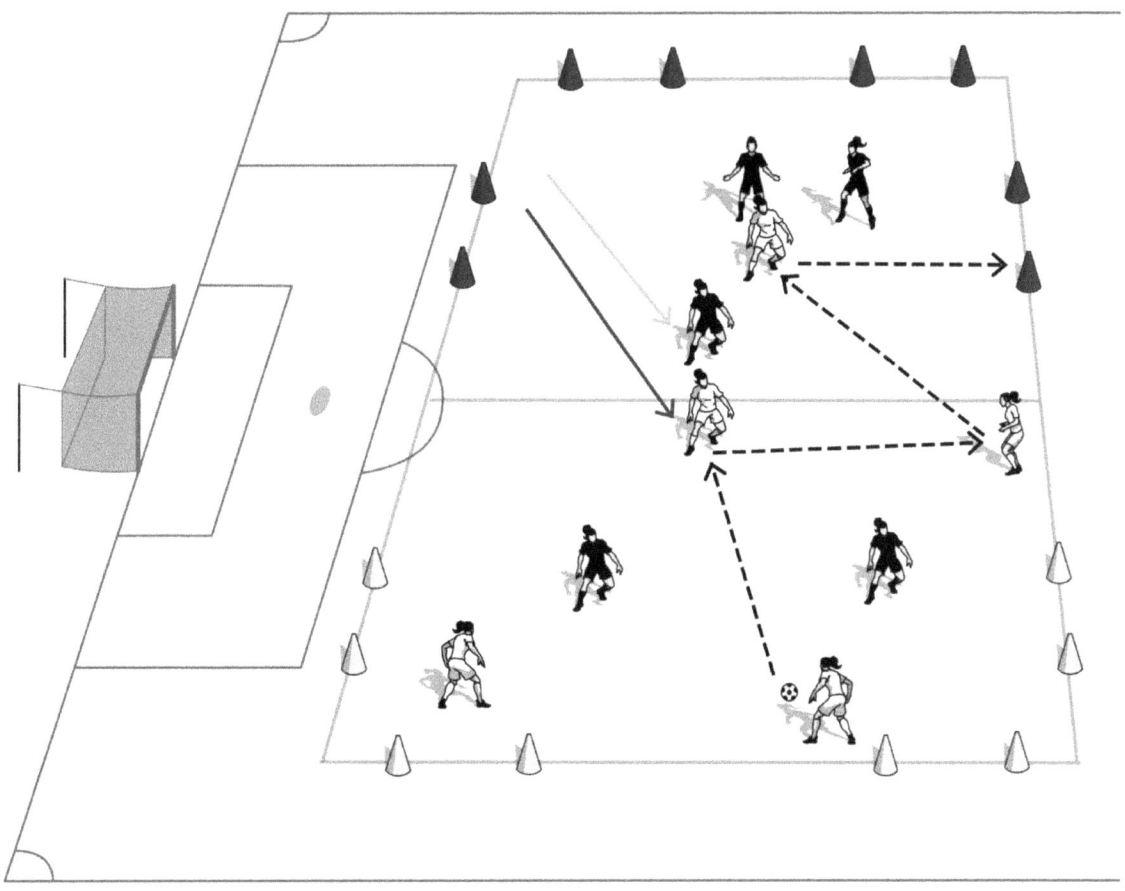

Conditions

- Each team must attack and defend four goals.
- Teams get one point for scoring in the wide goals, and three points for scoring in the end goals.

Progression

- A team cannot score in goals consecutively, forcing them to change the angle of attack.
- Once a goal has been scored in, it cannot be scored in again.
- Add an additional central goal.

Coaching Points

- Make the lines as compact as possible.
- A team must create balance between width and depth to defend goals.
- Force the opponent back and push them away from the goals.
- Make the opposition play in 'safe' areas.
- Make the opposition's play predictable.

11. Defending Central Areas

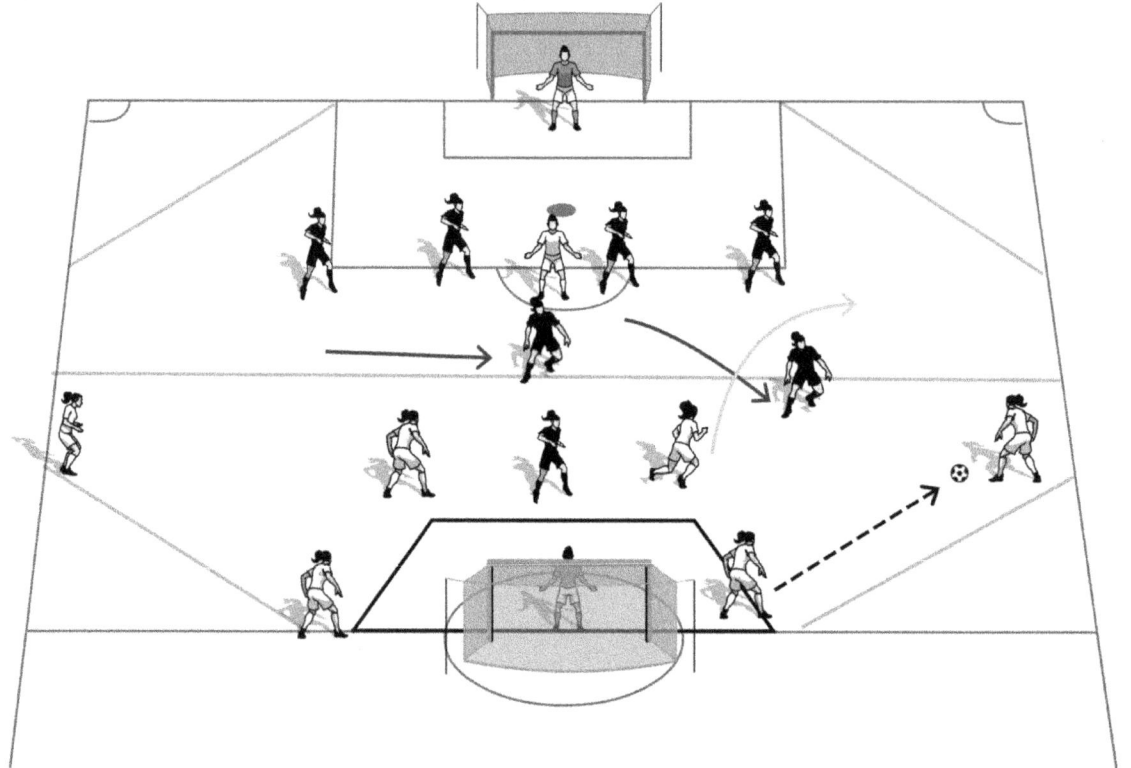

Conditions

- Play begins with goalkeepers in goal kick conditions.
- The defending team cannot drop into the penalty area before the ball arrives.
- This is an open game for the team in possession.
- The offside rule is in effect.

Progressions

- Force the defending team to start higher to create space in behind.
- Allow the attacking team to come outside the coned-off areas.

Coaching Points

- Remain compact as a unit.
- Protect the centre of the pitch.
- Force the opposition away from the central areas.
- Push the opposition out when clearing lines.

12. Advancing The Full-Backs

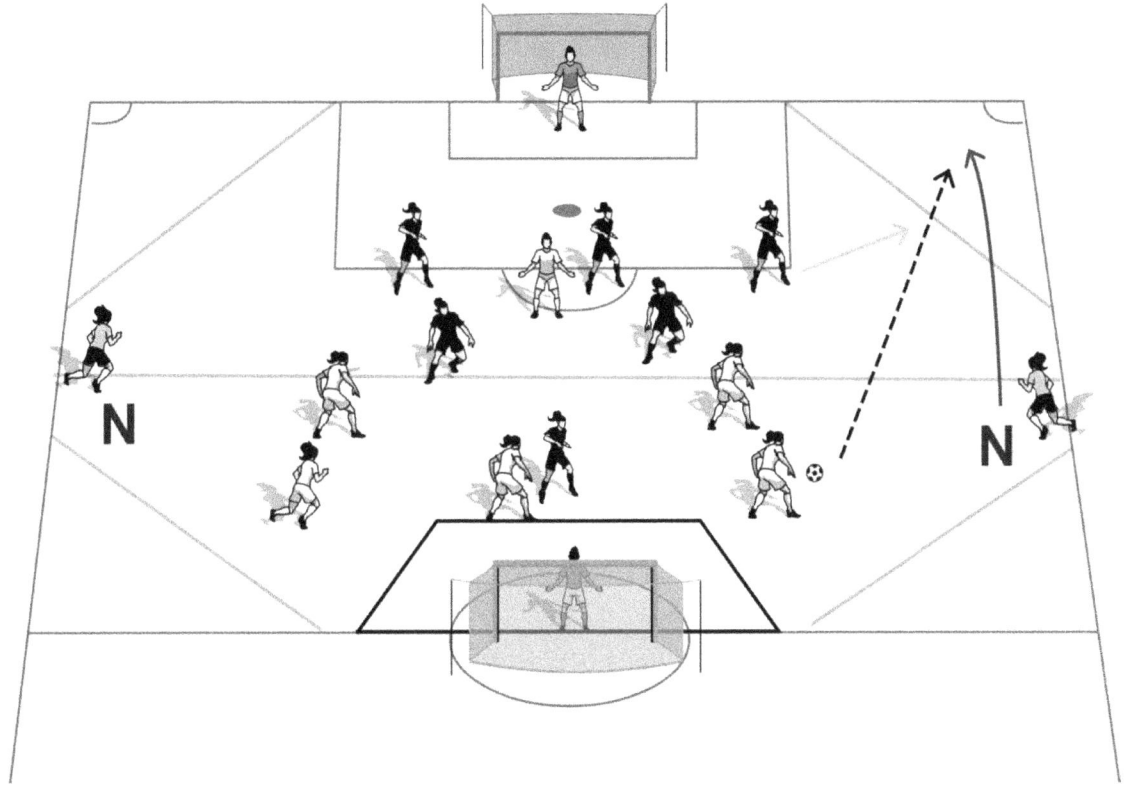

Conditions

- Two neutral players act as full-backs; these players are the only ones who can enter the corner end zones.
- Neutral players are limited to two touches.
- The team in possession looks to play passes into those wide areas.
- A team scores a goal after receiving a cross from one of the neutral players.

Progressions

- Allow defenders to enter wide areas to oppose the full-back.
- Remove zones and encourage the advancement of the full-back.

Coaching Points

- Timing the pass into the wide zone to meet the neutral players.
- Evasive movements from attacking players to create targets for crosses.
- Can we turn the opponent's back line to face their own goal?
- Encourage third-man runs from midfield.
- Changing the angle of attack.

10. In Possession – Final Third

"You never win if you don't attack."

Marcelo Bielsa

Pep Guardiola once said that it was his job to take the team two-thirds of the way up the field and the players the rest. While it probably helped that he had Lionel Messi at the time, he said his point focused on the importance of encouraging players to be fearless and creative in the final third. From the very beginning of his coaching career, Guardiola was always conscious that *overcoaching* in the attacking third would stifle his players' creativity and ability to improvise.

Of course, it was easy for him to say that when his front three was the aforementioned Messi, plus Thierry Henry and Samuel Eto'o, combined with the option to spend countless hours on the training ground to practise and perfect their combination play!

One of the most frequent questions we coaches get asked at training is, "Can we do some finishing practice?" However, whilst the above players have hours at practice, plus access to limitless facilities after practice to hone their finishing, it's slightly more challenging for grassroots coaches. One of the things I often tell my strikers is that the best players do their finishing practice after training. The likes of Harry Kane hone their skills by grabbing a coach, a youth team goalkeeper, a bag of balls and work on finishing until they've found what works best for them.

I remember my first attempts at doing finishing practices in large groups; lots of players stood around waiting their turn, with long gaps between turns and LOTS of fetching the ball. Finding the balance between repetition and realism is challenging because most of us aren't blessed with dozens of balls, multiple goals, and many goalkeepers willing to throw themselves about for the cause.

Sadly, we're not all blessed with coaching partners where we can split the players up and work in smaller groups. Often, as coaches, when we do manage to set up a finishing practice, we're so focused on getting the repetition or realism in, that we don't focus on the coaching points.

Though my personal preference for coaching finishing has become one-on-one sessions with strikers, you obviously cannot send 15 players home from training early to focus on individuals. As a result, I've always favoured position-specific games and game-related scenarios to ensure practice stays relevant and realistic, and gets as much repetition as possible.

To follow Pep's lead, I also want my players to be creative and free-thinking in the final third. One of the things I tell my players is that there is no incorrect way to score a goal. A 30-yard rocket counts just the same as a 15-pass move with a one-yard tap-in. Likewise, a miskicked effort that takes two deflections on its way in is also a goal. To quote Yogi Berra, "It only counts as one!" So, whilst I think it's important that there is the freedom to improvise, I like to base practice on a simple structure where everyone understands each teammate's movements.

A final reminder of our in possession principles:

- Make the pitch as big as we can
- Attack the space created
- Play the safest, most direct pass
- Find the free player
- Play around or through the press

Our additional sub-principles for the final third are:

1. Width in the attacking line
2. Third-man runs from midfield
3. Direct passes that penetrate
4. Be creative
5. Retain possession when the opposition is in good shape

Make The Pitch As Big As We Can

As we move up the pitch, and the opposition drops and narrows to protect the goal, it's going to be much tougher to find space to play in. The defending team are going to work their hardest to protect the area in front of their goal and deny space in behind as well as in between their lines.

We, as a team, want to counteract this by trying to stretch the play across their back line to force them to cover and defend a bigger space. We want to maximise the space we use to force the defending team to try to cover that space (Figure 1) and give them a decision to make.

By stretching the play, defenders may be drawn out of position to close down the free player, leaving gaps in their defensive structure. This can create opportunities for other attacking players to exploit those spaces and receive the ball in advantageous positions.

A really popular move for Liverpool under Jurgen Klopp has been for the wingers to hug the touchline as wide as they can, forcing the defence to try to get as tight as possible to the wide player, thus allowing deeper runs in the half-space from Trent Alexander-Arnold or Andrew Robinson to attack.

Similarly, Pep Guardiola also loved having Riyad Mahrez stretch the play to create room for Kevin De Bruyne to attack in central areas.

Attack The Space Created

If we're successful in stretching the opposition's back line to trigger defensive movement, this will destabilise their compact shape. Once achieved, we want to ensure we're exploiting the newly created space. Ideally, in a perfect world, our movement has opened up the defence directly in front of goal and allowed our striker the freedom to race through and score.

However, if the opposition remain compact centrally, we would look to play around their block to try and penetrate the final third in wide areas and get the winger ❼ on the ball. This can look one of two ways, either to play outside of the full-back (Figure 1) or to invite the full-back out and look to play in behind them (Figure 2).

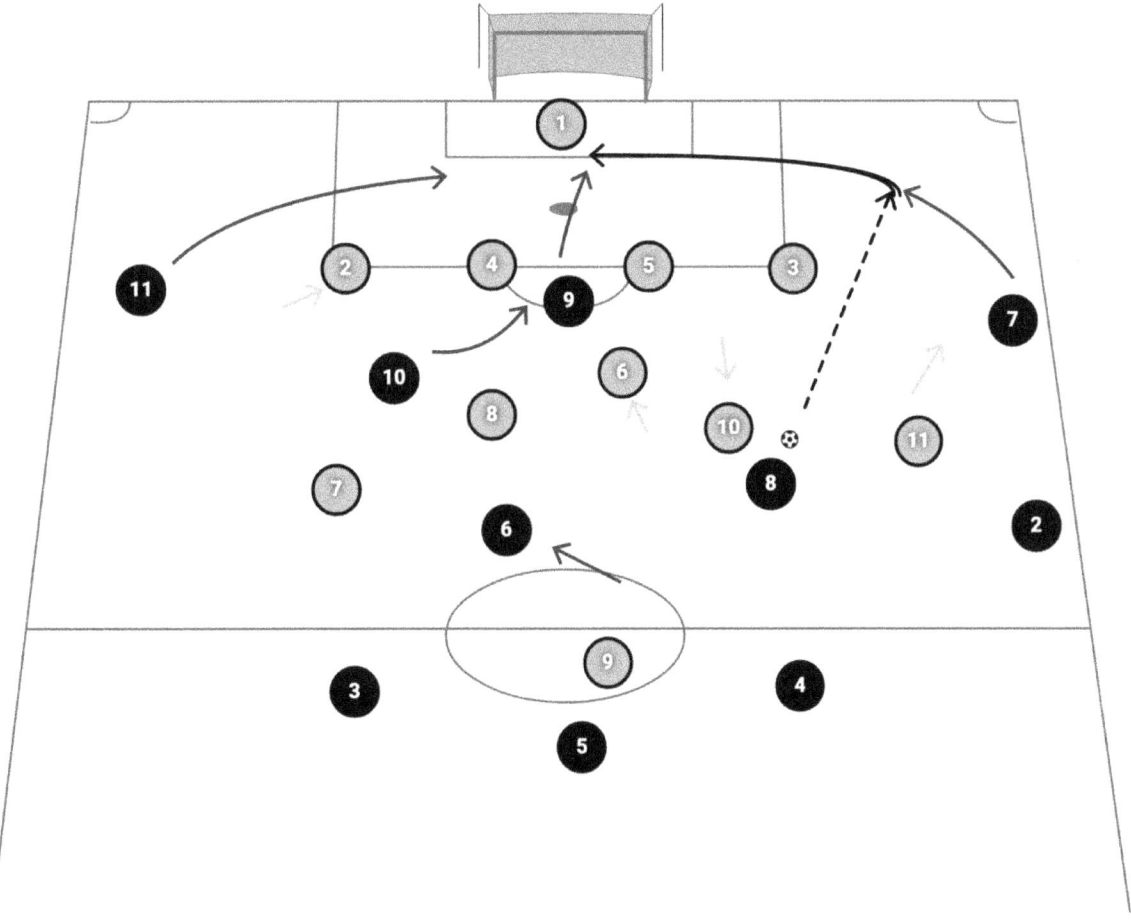

Figure 1 – Compact full-back, pass outside to winger.

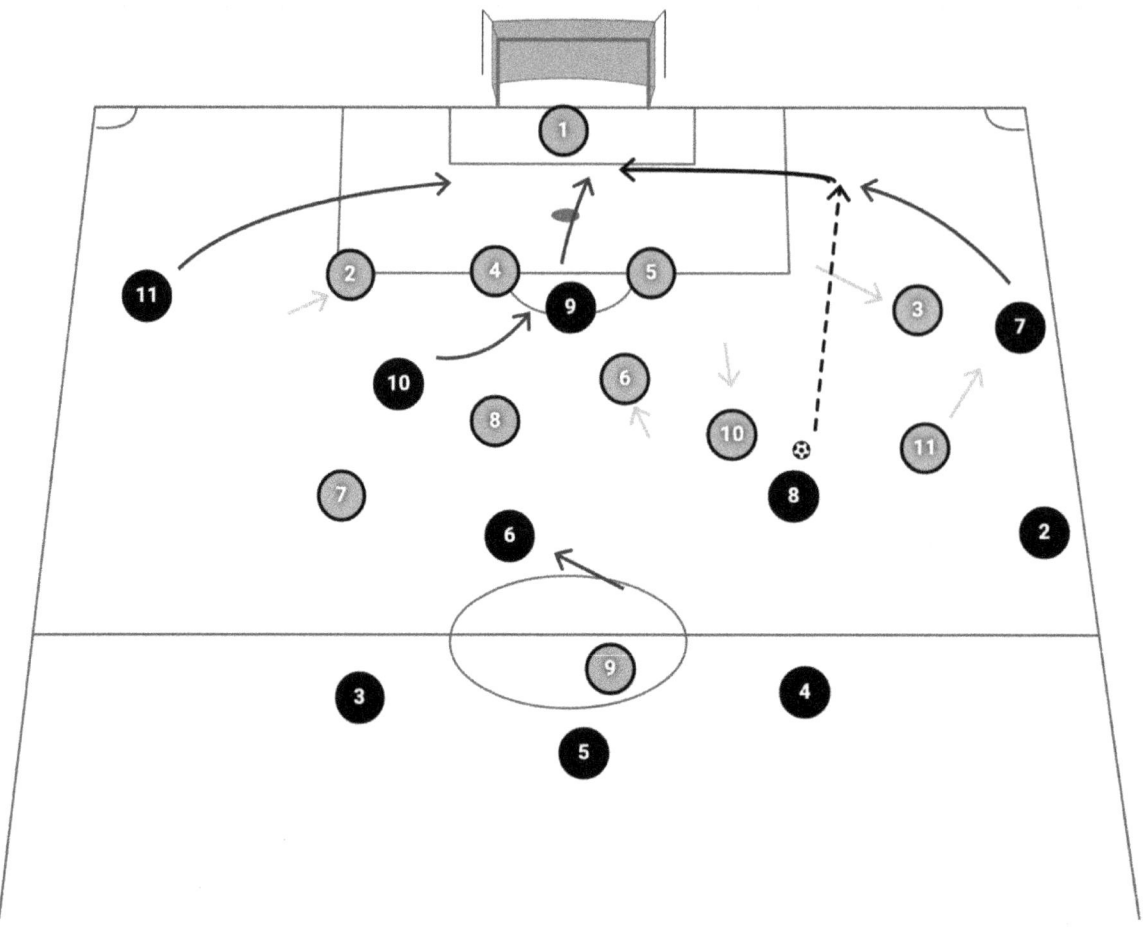

Figure 2 – Isolated full-back, pass in behind.

If we're successful in getting the winger in behind, we'd then look for the forward ❾ the opposite winger and at least one of the midfielders ❿ to fill the box to provide targets and get on the end of a cross.

Play The Safest, Most Direct Pass

It is important – in the final third – that we're making penetrative passes in an attempt to unlock the opponent's low block. We also have to accept that there is an increased likelihood of surrendering possession. As coaches, if we're overcautious in the final third and pass this message to the players, it can stifle creativity and players may focus on ball retention over chance creation. Despite this, we still want to avoid horizontal passes to prevent the opposition from mounting quick counterattacks.

Vertical passes from midfield ❽ into spaces between defensive lines can really damage any defensive shape as they can force the defending team to turn and face their own goal. In these instances, they're forced to focus not just on the player that they're marking but also on the area that the ball is travelling into. In such circumstances, the advantage can be with the attacker whose body shape is pointing towards the goal (Figure 3).

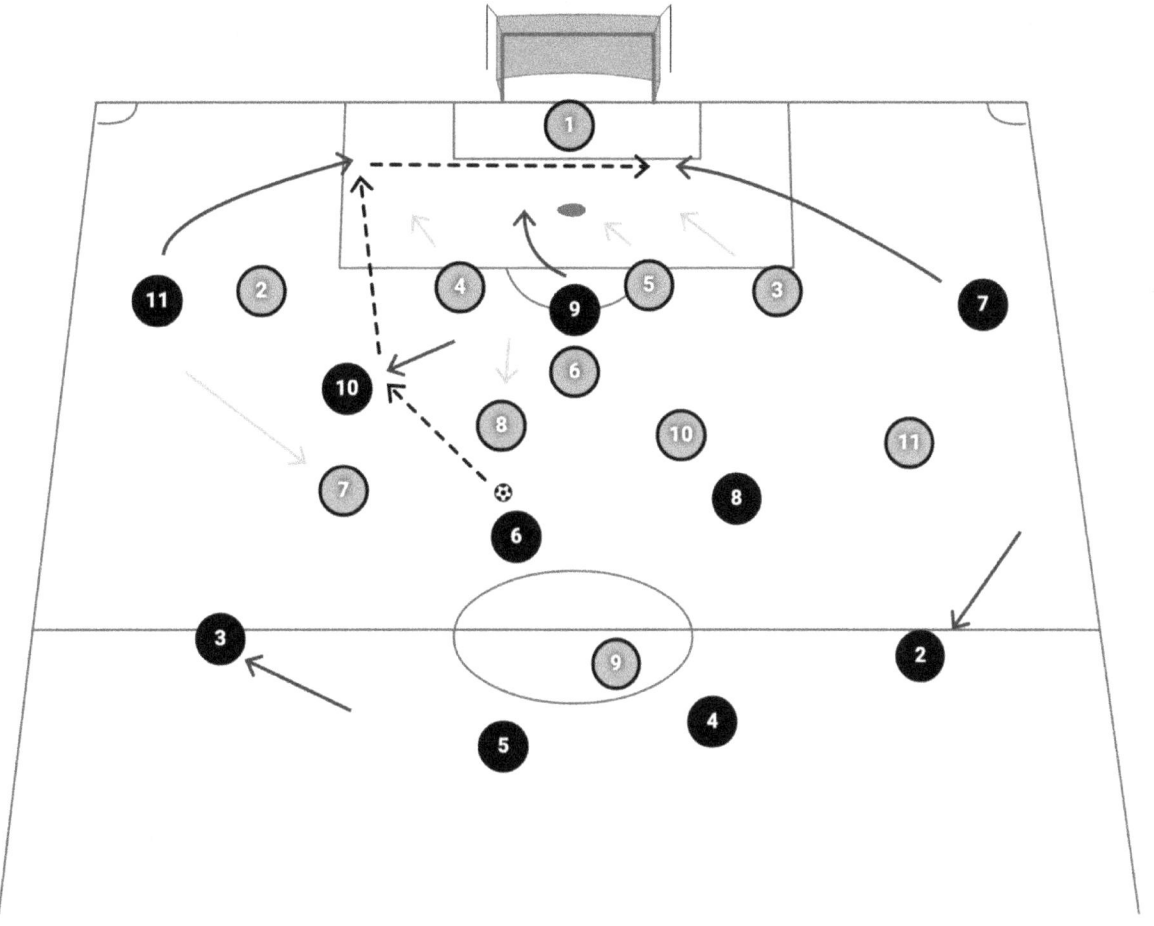

Figure 3 – Pass into the half space.

Find The Free Player

In crowded areas, it can be challenging to create scoring chances, especially as the attacking team are working harder to attack space than the opposition is in defending it. However, by locating the free player, a team can exploit pockets of space and time in the opponent's defence. Off-the-ball movement is so vital in evading a marker and creating the freedom to receive the ball. That off-the-ball movement will prevent the defending team from settling and allow us to set the tempo.

An effective way to unbalance an opponent is to encourage third-man runs from midfield lines to create overloads between defensive lines. For example, the outside central midfielder **10** playing a direct pass behind the full-back can release the winger to get a low ball across goal for the attacking line **9** / **7** to get on the end of it (Figure 3). Alternatively, we can look to destabilise the defensive line and play in behind them, getting passes in behind for the forward **9** (Figure 4).

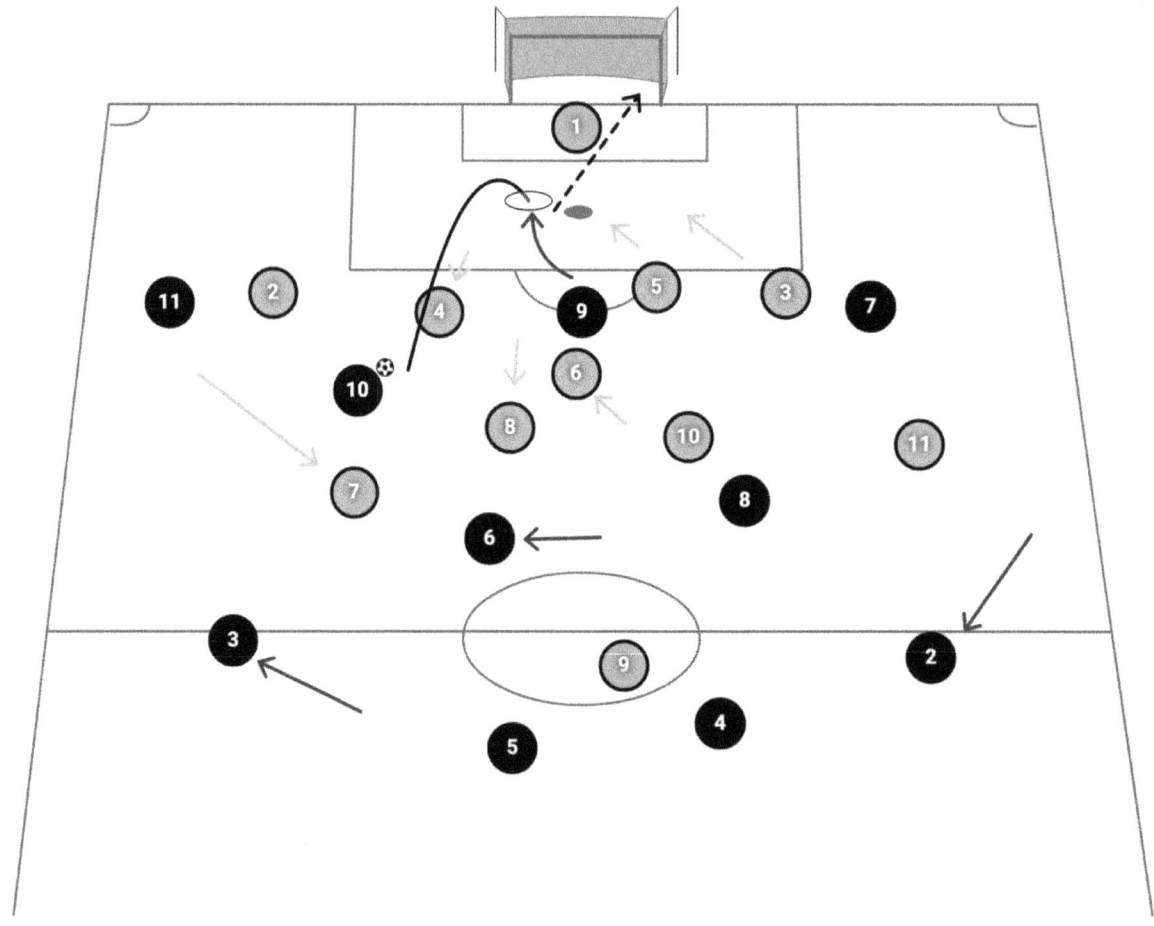

Figure 4 – Pass in behind for the striker.

Additionally, it's important that we maintain a free player in supporting roles. If our winger is in possession, we want to make sure the full-back ❸ / ❷ or the outside centre midfielder ❿ / ❽ joins them to prevent the ball carrier being overloaded by the opposition full-back and winger.

Play Around Or Through The Press

When we are in the attacking third, the opponent's primary focus is defensive duties and protecting the goal. However, they will still be looking to force the attacking team into preferred areas in which to regain possession and launch a counterattack.

One of the strengths of Mikel Arteta's Arsenal side has been to play through a low block by having their striker start high to pin in the centre-backs but rapidly drop off to encourage the defenders to follow in tandem with Bakayo Saka or Gabrielle Martinelli rotating to fill that space before the ball is slipped inside. Likewise, Harry Kane, at Spurs, was a master of the ability to separate himself from the defender, "drop and spin", just in time for the ball to be played in behind by Heung-Min Son as the defender stepped out to cover Kane.

In addition to being penetrative in the final third, we also want to maintain the ability to retain possession in areas that the opposition doesn't occupy. If their line is compact around the penalty area, we want to maintain the ability to move the ball back out into deeper areas to force them to step out and engage with the ball carrier. If we can invite them out successfully, that would provide us with an area of space to target.

Conclusion

There are an unlimited number of combinations and scenarios that could unfold in the final third for scoring a goal or creating a goalscoring opportunity. The aim of this chapter is to present a basic framework for a team's structure in the final third, from which the team forms a basic understanding that they can build. It's important that we do not stifle the creativity of players, but *especially* so in the final third.

We always want to try to play to the strengths of our players. Whilst some sides have great success scoring goals in a certain way, defending teams will eventually figure them out.

In my first season as a Head Coach, our primary method of scoring goals was to play the ball behind the full-back down one wing as the opposite side's winger raced towards the box (down the opposite side's wing) before slotting home at the far post. I called it the 'Sterling to Sane' goal (despite my players having no idea who either of them were), and it was how we scored goals. If teams were able to figure us out – by stopping the through ball or by blocking the cross – we were a team with no plan B.

The most successful sides have the ability to score all different kinds of goals as they adapt to the challenge the opposition poses in front of them. Gradually, as I evolved as a coach, I was able to develop a system so that we had multiple ways of creating goalscoring opportunities, depending on what the opposition allowed us or prevented us from doing.

11. Out of Possession – Defensive Third

"Defending well is the ability to control spaces.
If the space is big, I will suffer."

Sergio Busquets

For any successful team, the ability not to concede goals is as important as scoring goals. In previous chapters, we've looked at trying to prevent the opponent from building up to create a goalscoring opportunity. In this chapter, we focus on the importance of simply preventing goals.

We often think about defending in our defensive third as a last resort, something that teams who are regular visitors to the Emirates, Etihad, or Nou Camp might employ. However, we have to consider that sometimes the opposition will do good things and penetrate our defensive third. In these instances, we want to prevent goalscoring opportunities first, and delay goalscoring opportunities second.

In these circumstances, it's tempting to say it's about putting your body on the line and protecting the goal at all costs. However, there is a greater benefit to having a clearly defined game plan for how to defend in front of your own goal. Often, the sides who protect the area in front of their own goal best are the ones who are patient and organised.

A final reminder of our defensive principles:

- Remain as compact as possible
- Leave the furthest player
- Protect the middle of the field
- Let the opposition play in safe areas
- Make the opposition's play predictable

The sub-principles for defending in the final third:

1. Horizontal shifting as a unit to close gaps
2. Position defenders to block passing options
3. Protect the central areas in front of goal
4. Force the opposition's attacks towards wide areas
5. Anticipate the opposition's passing patterns

Remain As Compact As Possible

When we're defending, it is crucial that we defend the space in front of our goal. To do this, organisation is essential and remaining as compact as possible prevents the opposition from occupying gaps between our defensive lines. Additionally, it is critical that – as the opposition move and recycle the ball – we are able to shift horizontally as a single unit whilst protecting the space.

When the ball is in central areas, we want to narrow up and ensure that the opposition cannot play in between the lines (Figure 1).

David Moye's West Ham are a superb example of this, as they're willing to get bodies around the penalty area in a block of four and five and absorb pressure by denying their opponents space using Edson Alvarez and James Ward-Prowse as defensive screens in front of Thomas Soucek, whilst Lucas Paqueta and Jarrod Bowen narrow. This forces their opponents to play in areas of the field that West Ham are happy to let them play in; attempts to penetrate are met by overloads of defenders.

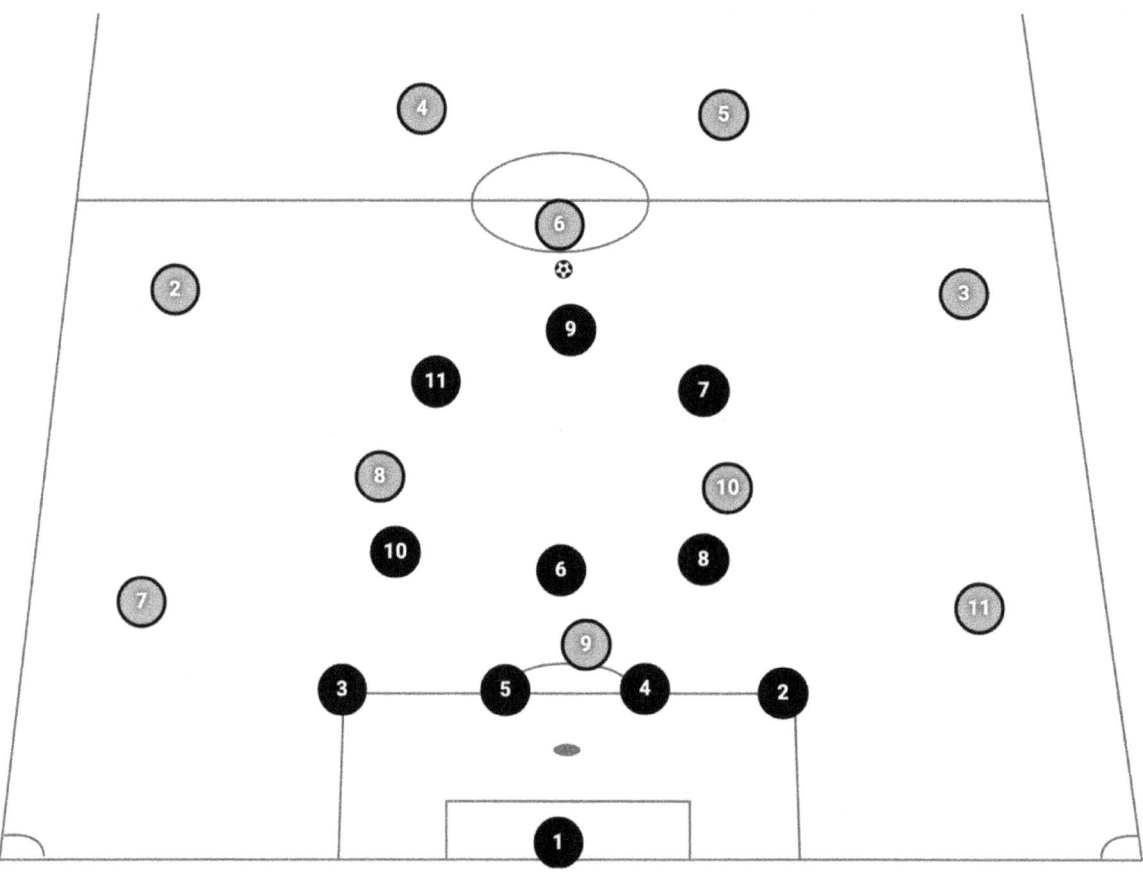

Figure 1 – Defending centrally, balanced shape.

Leave The Furthest Player

When we're in the own third – without the ball – we have to prioritise and understand who the biggest threat to our goal is at that present moment. In this case, it's the player in possession and the players immediately around that player. It is important that we position our defenders to prevent shooting options and block or disrupt passing options to the furthest player. Our aim, in this instance, is to prevent the opposition from making penetrating passes.

As the ball is moved from central areas, and the opposition look to create an overload, we shuffle across to put pressure on the ball whilst making sure we cover the space in behind (Figure 2). The winger ❼ moves across to put pressure on the ball and prevent balls being played inside; the near side full-back ❸ will move across to mark the winger in front of the ball whilst the opposite full-back ❷ will swing around to act as an extra central defender to protect the penalty area.

The players furthest away from the ball may still pose a threat to our goal, but they are not an immediate danger. As part of our defensive strategy, we must either look to cut off passing options to these players or shift our block accordingly, when they receive the ball.

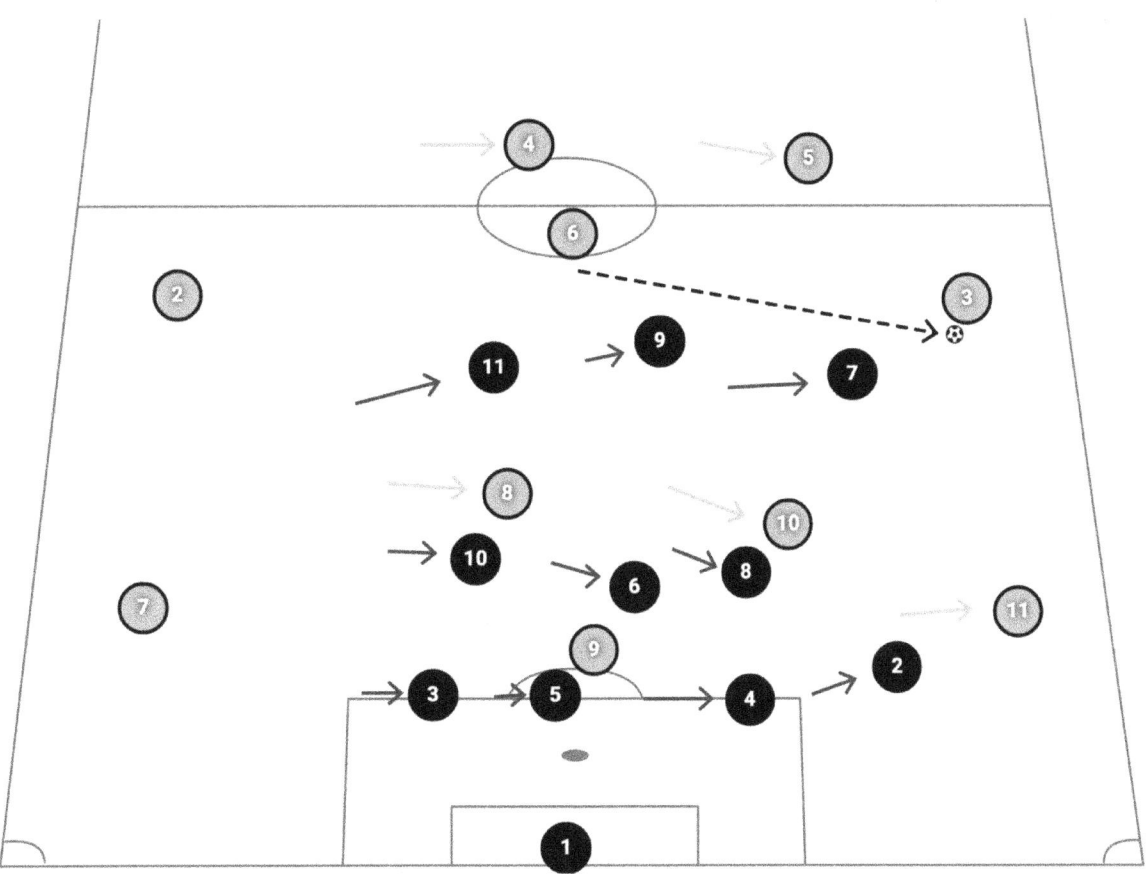

Figure 2 – Defending on the wing, leaving the furthest players.

Protect The Middle Of The Field

Attacking teams typically wish to attack in central areas because this provides a higher percentage scoring opportunity. The narrower the angle to goal, the lower the likelihood of a goal. As such, the possession team will look to find ways to trigger our press and encourage defenders to step out of shape to exploit the newly created space by trying to pull our central defenders out of the back line.

Whenever we are defending, we have to make a decision – as a team – about when to protect the goal and when to look to regain possession. In the defensive third, one non-negotiable we need to maintain is that we must always look to protect central areas. If we have defenders positioned in front of goal, they can block shots, intercept passes, and (if needed) make tackles to prevent the opposing team from getting clear shots on goal.

For the attacking side, central areas of the field are often used as passing channels to create goalscoring opportunities. By defending centrally, you can cut off these passing lanes, forcing the opposition to play more difficult and riskier passes. This increases the chances of intercepting the ball or forcing turnovers.

Let The Opposition Play In Safe Areas.

When we are defending, we have to let the opposition play *somewhere*, so that we can be in a position to regain possession. If we're compact and protecting central areas, we don't want to risk surrendering that by looking to 'nick' the ball back in these areas. Instead, we want to push the opposition into wide areas before looking to regain possession (Figure 3).

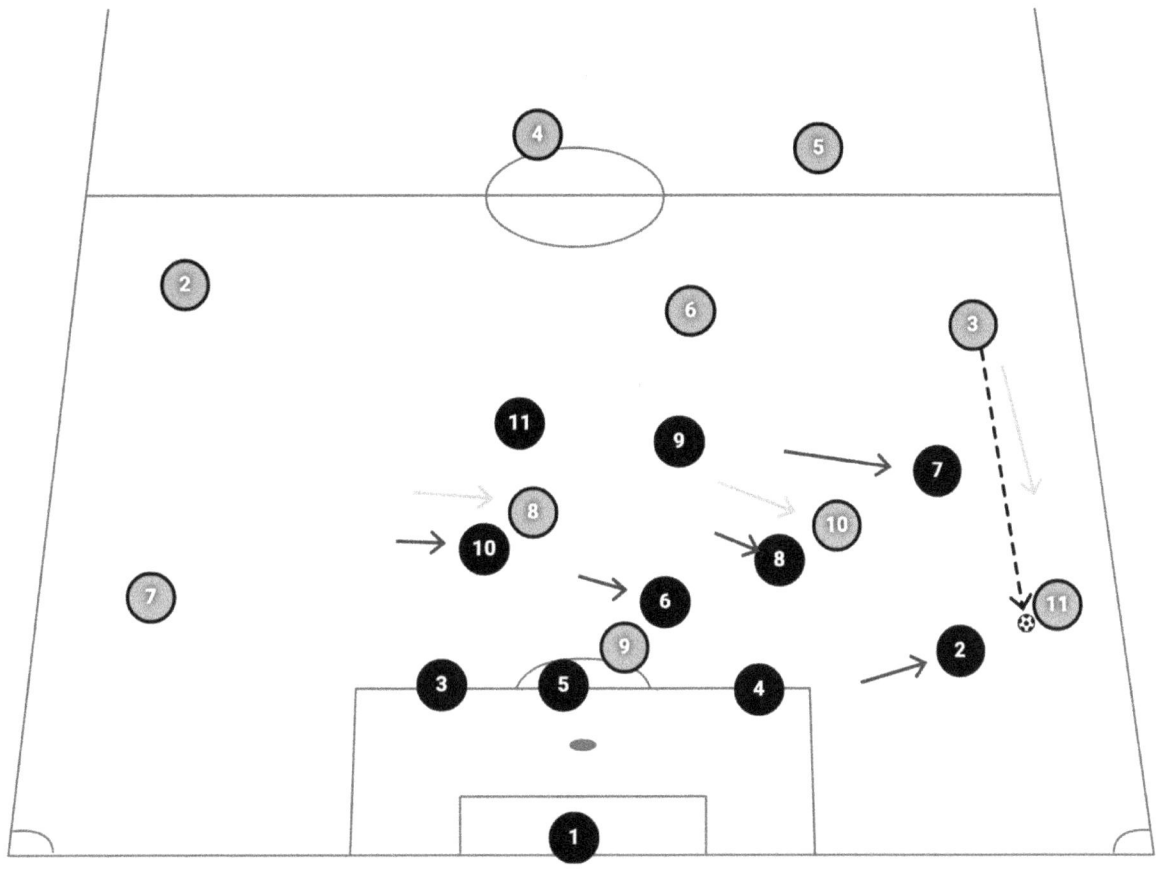

Figure 3 – Putting pressure on the ball to regain possession.

Again, the full-back ❸ moves across to exert pressure, whilst the outside central midfielder ❽ looks to cover the passing option inside. This then allows the winger ❼ to drop and cut off the passing line, either to the inside player or the supporting full-back, thus isolating the winger.

We want to do this – in these areas – because the angle to goal is narrower, reducing the risk of a direct shot on goal. In turn, the touchline acts as an additional defender, putting the attacking team under more pressure. If we're able to isolate the player in possession, this will allow us to attempt to regain possession and launch a counterattack.

Make The Opposition's Play Predictable

In the final third, making the opposition predictable is a means of limiting their creativity. Predictable play makes it harder for the opposing team to find their key players and they must potentially rely on individual brilliance or unexpected moments of creativity. When you can anticipate their actions, you can stifle their creative players and force them into making foreseeable and less effective decisions. This reduces the overall threat posed by the opposition and increases your team's chances of successfully defending. Additionally, you can help force your opponents into mistakes through mental frustration or trying to force the ball through your defensive shape.

When the opposition's play is predictable, it becomes easier for your team to anticipate their moves and adjust defensively. This allows your defenders to position themselves effectively, close down passing lanes, and mark opposing players more efficiently. Predictability helps maintain a solid defensive structure and reduces the chances of conceding goals.

When you can predict their moves, you can position your players to intercept passes or win the ball in specific areas (Figure 4). This allows your team to quickly transition from defence to attack and exploit the spaces left behind by the predictable opposition.

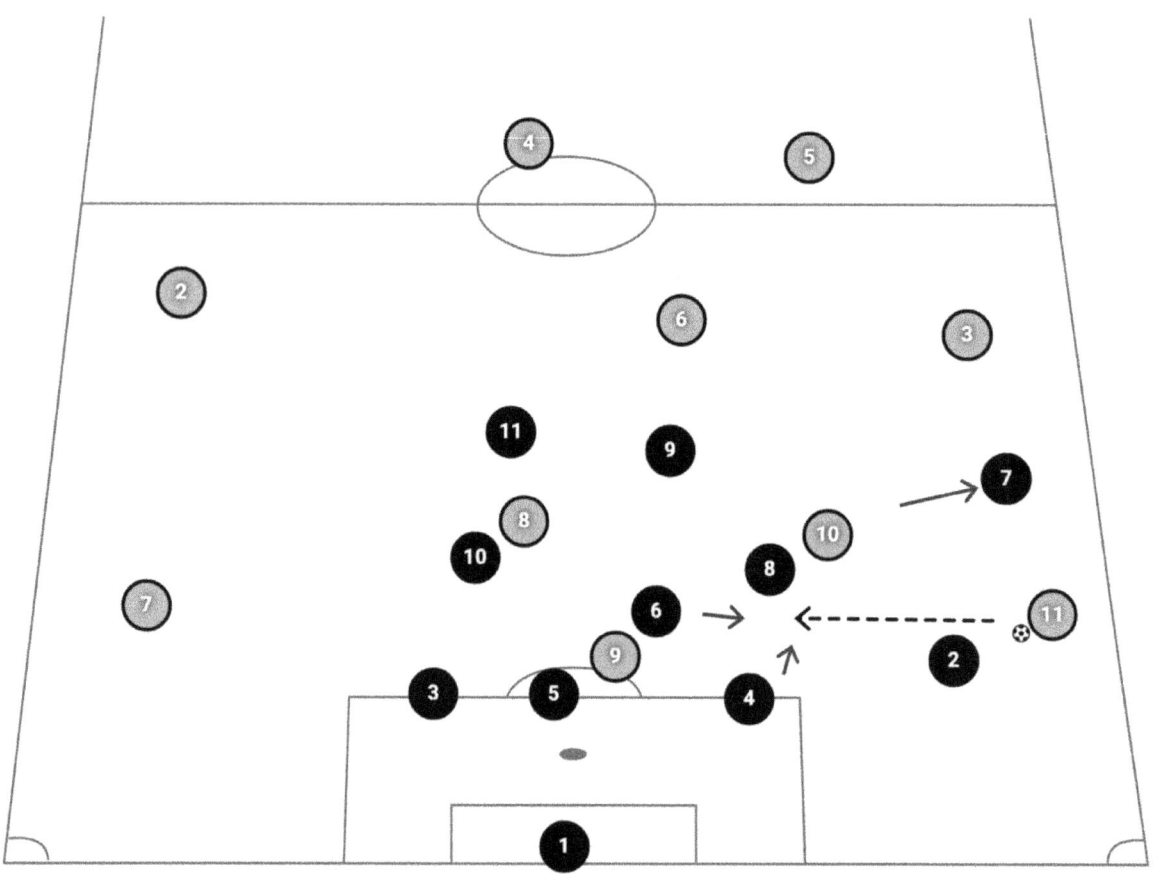

Figure 4 – Successful interception through defensive overload.

Conclusion

Defending in the final third doesn't always have to be about last-gasp tackles or heroic saves to prevent a certain goal. Having solid defensive principles in front of goal brings multiple benefits, including defensive organisation, limiting creativity, effective pressing, tactical adjustments and even counterattacking opportunities.

Additionally, a good defensive shape requires less energy to defend at a point when your opponent is expending the majority of theirs.

Despite not having the ball and having an unfavourable field position, if we have a clear and solid plan, we are still able to deny the opposition long enough to force them to return the ball to us.

12. Final Third Practices

In this chapter, we look at the practices for attacking in the final third and defending in front of our own goal. This chapter is slightly different to the others as I've tried to provide practices that focus on finishing but which also include pitch geography. Where I have used a half-pitch, these practices can still be refined down to the space and the number of players at your disposal.

The coaching points can be amended, based on how the coach sees fit, in terms of their aims and the needs of the players. The same practice can have many different coaching points based on *your* needs.

Key

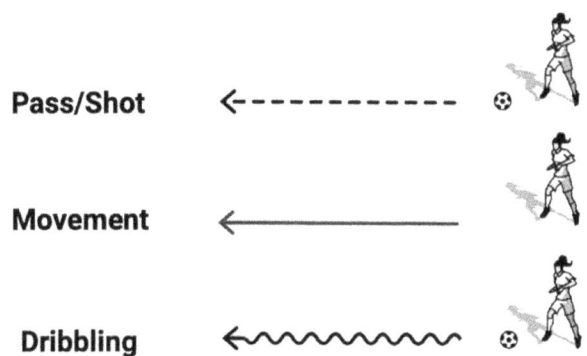

Reminders

- Throughout these practices, where I have included goalkeepers, this is to demonstrate how they can be used in the practice. If there are no goalkeepers, then they can be substituted for a mini goal or gate with a condition such as a 'two touch finish'.
- I have used the same number of players throughout the practices for uniformity, but have designed them so they can be adjusted for 8-18 players. If you are working with an odd number of players, working with a neutral player or 'magic player' should not impact the realism of the practice too greatly.
- Where I have used multiple goals or poles, this is to demonstrate the target that players are aiming to play to or through. Where mini goals or poles are unavailable, I would use cones in their place.
- Pitch size and timings have been deliberately left off; this is because you will know what works best for your players.

1. Creating Overloads In The Final Third

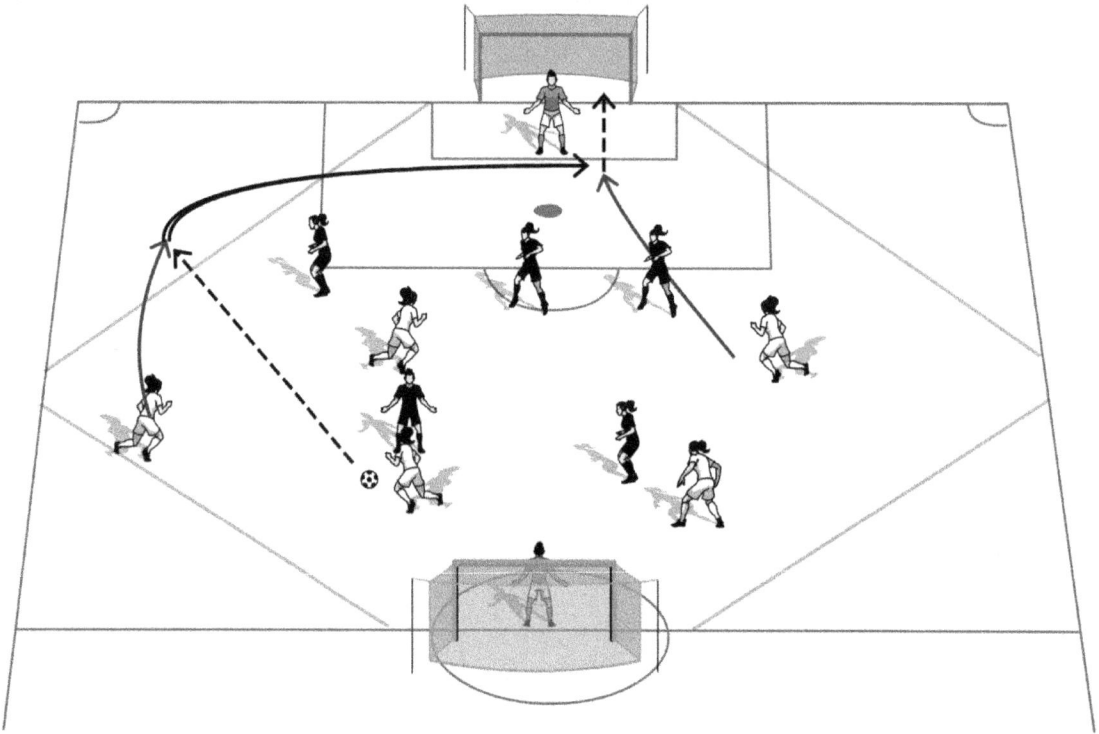

Conditions

- Corner areas are coned off, but the game remains open in central areas.
- One player from each team can enter the corner areas to stretch the attack.

Progressions

- Progress to two attackers and one defender allowed in the corner areas.
- Progress to three attackers and two defenders.
- Remove the zones; reinforce the coaching points.

Coaching Points

- Can we get runners ahead of the ball and stretch the play?
- Can we look to exploit the free space with crosses into central areas?
- Can we attack the goal with numbers?
- Can we turn defenders and get them to face their own goal?

2. Pull-Back Crosses

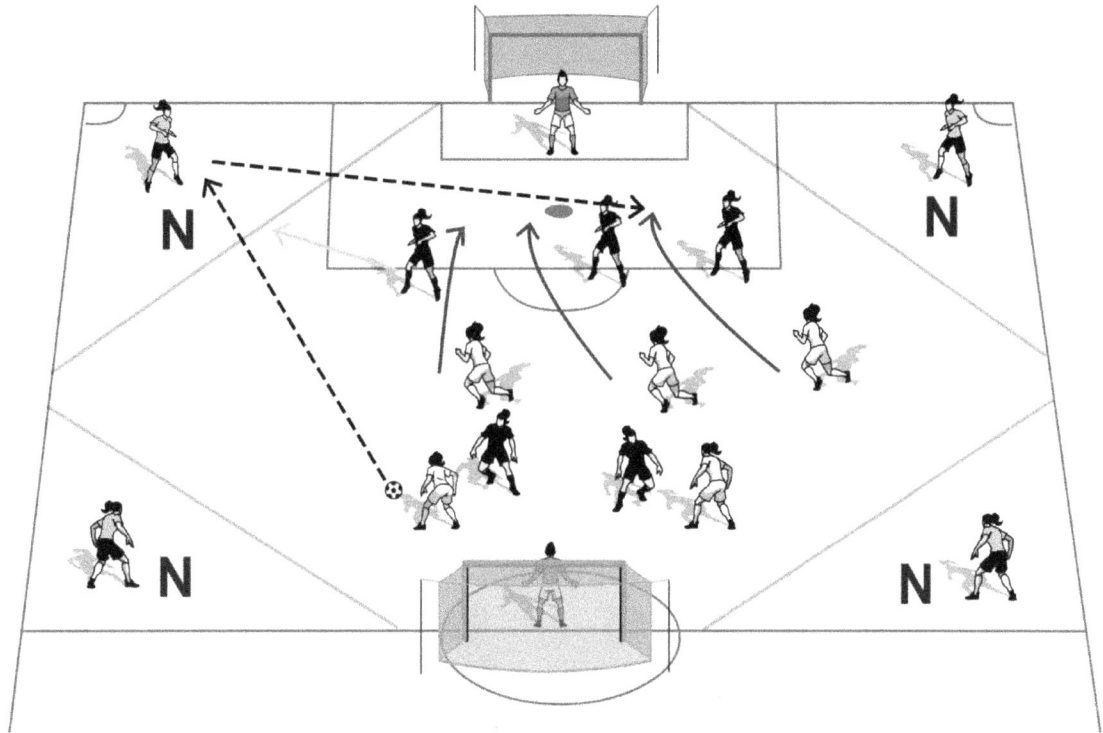

Conditions

- Play starts with the goalkeeper.
- Neutral players act as full-backs in the defensive half and wingers in the attacking half.
- The ball must be played out wide to an attacking player before any attempt to score can be made. Neutral players can pass to one another.

Progression

- Neutral players must link to central players to break lines.
- Make neutral players opposed.

Coaching Points

- Can the attacking neutral players advance and narrow for pull-back crosses?
- Can the attackers make runs across the defender/goalkeeper?
- Can the midfield make third-man runs into the final third?
- Encourage off-the-ball movement to confuse the opponent.
- Out of Possession – Can we block the cross? Do we defend the near post?
- Out of Possession – Pick up players and track third-man runners.
- Out of Possession – Defend the central area.

3. Transitional Finishing Game

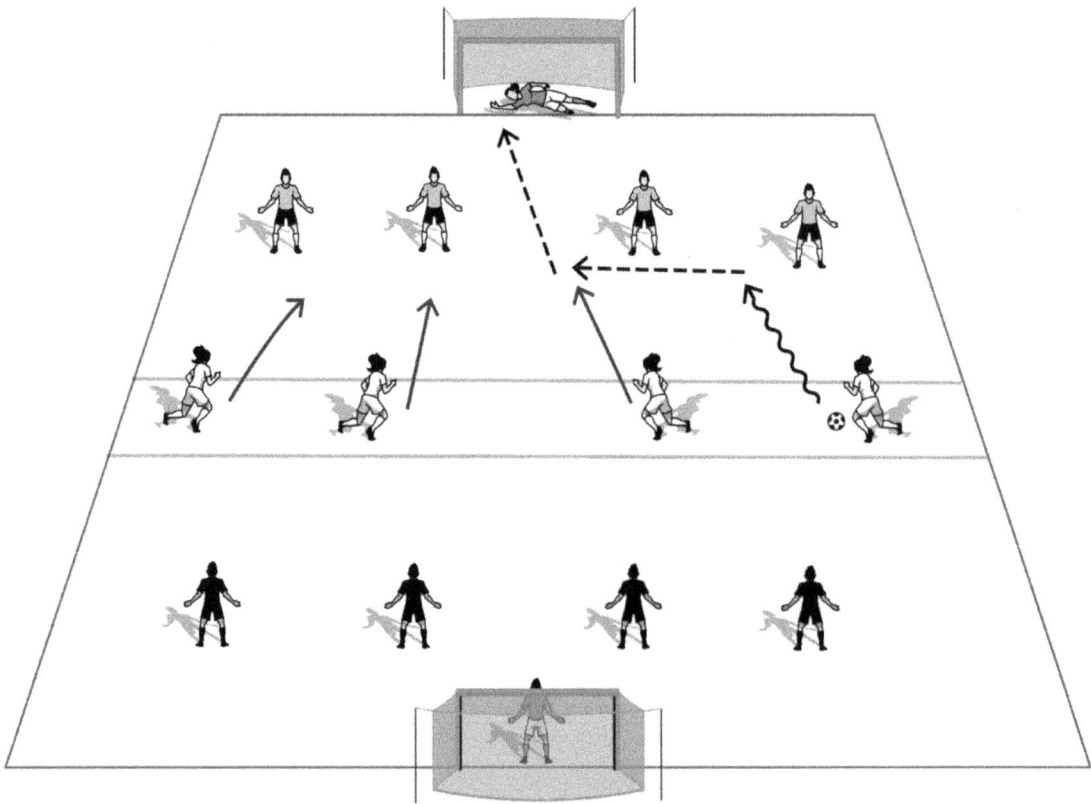

Conditions

- One team starts in possession and looks to attack one of the goals.
- If the team scores, they receive another ball and attack the opposite goal.
- If the possession team fails to score, they are replaced by the defending team, who look to attack the opposite goal.

Progressions

- Add a shot clock to increase the speed of play.

Coaching Points

- Create the space early and exploit it quickly.
- Break lines and force the opposition to defend in bad areas.
- Have runners ahead of the ball.
- Out of Possession – remain compact to deny space.
- Out of Possession – protect central areas.
- Out of Possession – force the opposition away from goal.

4. Combining Third-Man Runs With Centre Forward Play

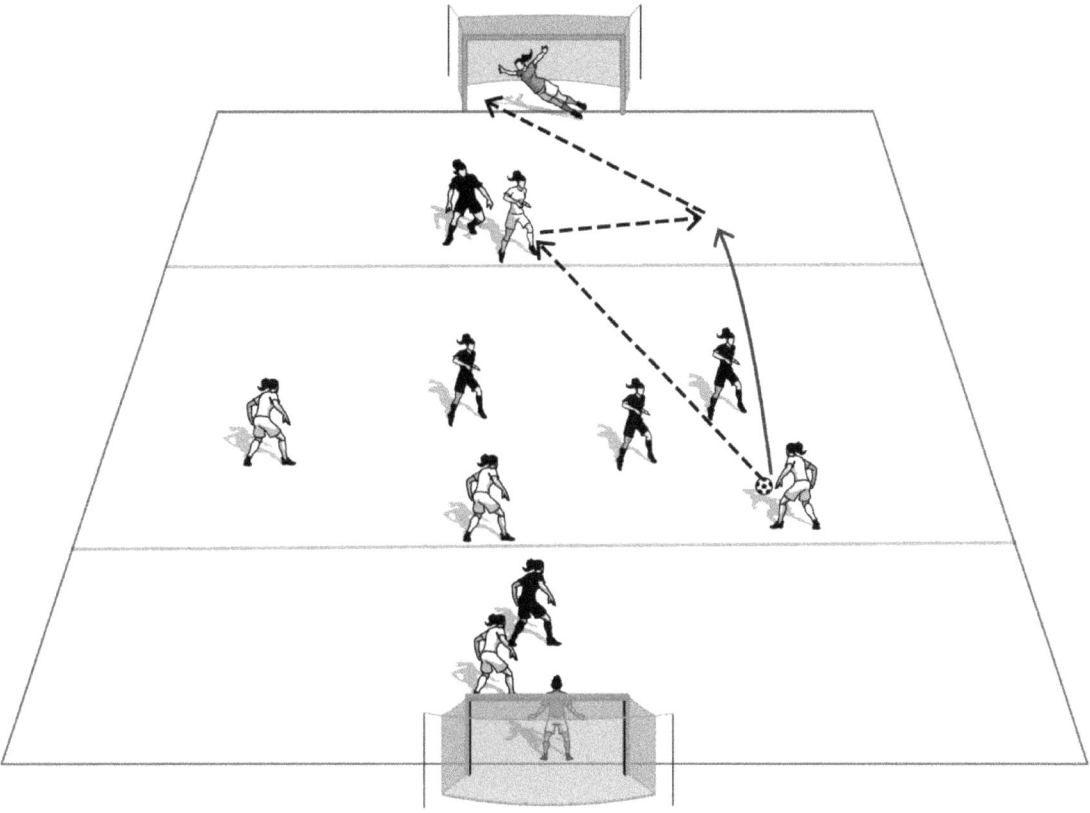

Conditions

- Three zones. One striker and one defender are restricted to each end zone.
- An open game in central areas where the possession team aims to pass into their striker and create 2v1 overloads.
- The attacking team keeps possession if they score.

Progression

- Allow additional attackers and defenders into the final third to create a 3v2 overload.
- Remove restrictions; encourage forward movements to create overloads.

Coaching Points

- Maximise the space quickly to create passing lanes for direct passes.
- Anticipation of forward passes to join attacks and create overloads.
- Encourage creative movement in the final third.
- Out of Possession – can we block vertical passes?
- Out of Possession – pick up players and track third-man runners.

5. Scoring In The Final Third

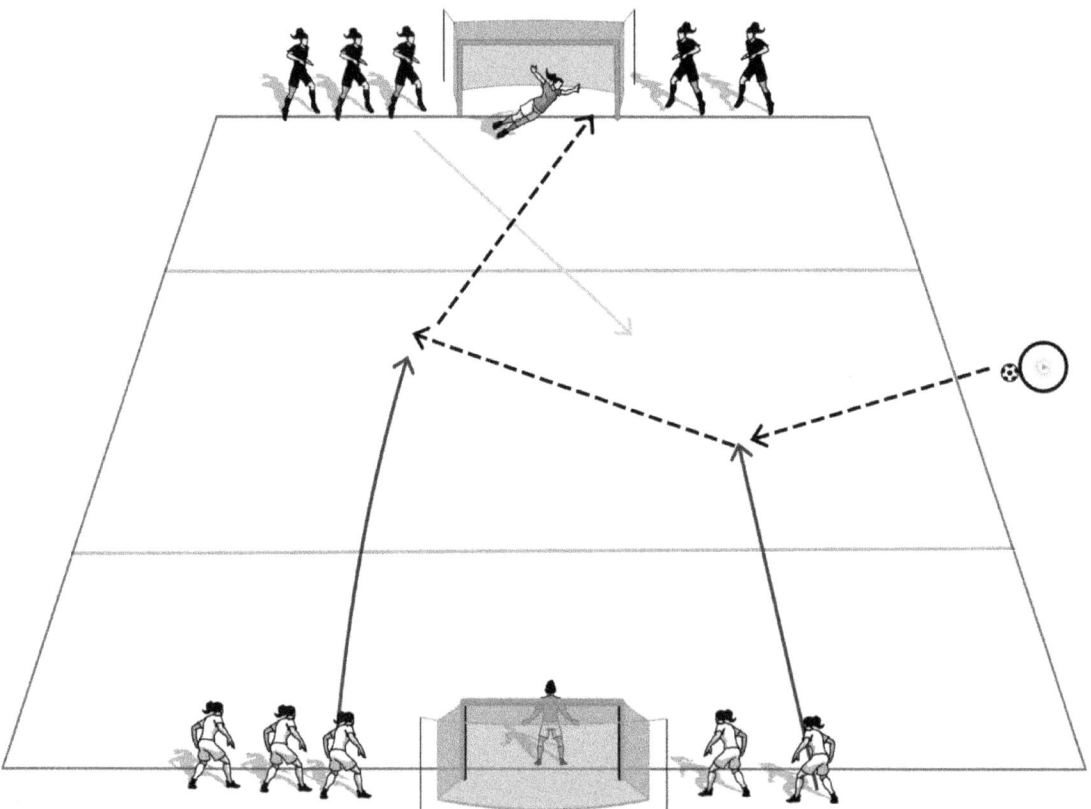

Conditions

- One team starts in possession with a 1v1 against the goalkeeper.
- After an attempt on goal, the opposing team has two players join as they look to create a 2v1 overload and seek to create a goalscoring opportunity of their own.
- The two teams alternate until all players are in the game.

Progression

- Players must score in the attacking zone.

Coaching Points

- Encourage movement off-the-ball.
- Stretch the play to isolate defenders.
- Aim to shoot from central areas.
- Commit players in forward areas when crossing.
- Out of Possession – can we slow down the attack?
- Out of Possession – can we force attacks away from goal?

6. Breaking Down A Low Block

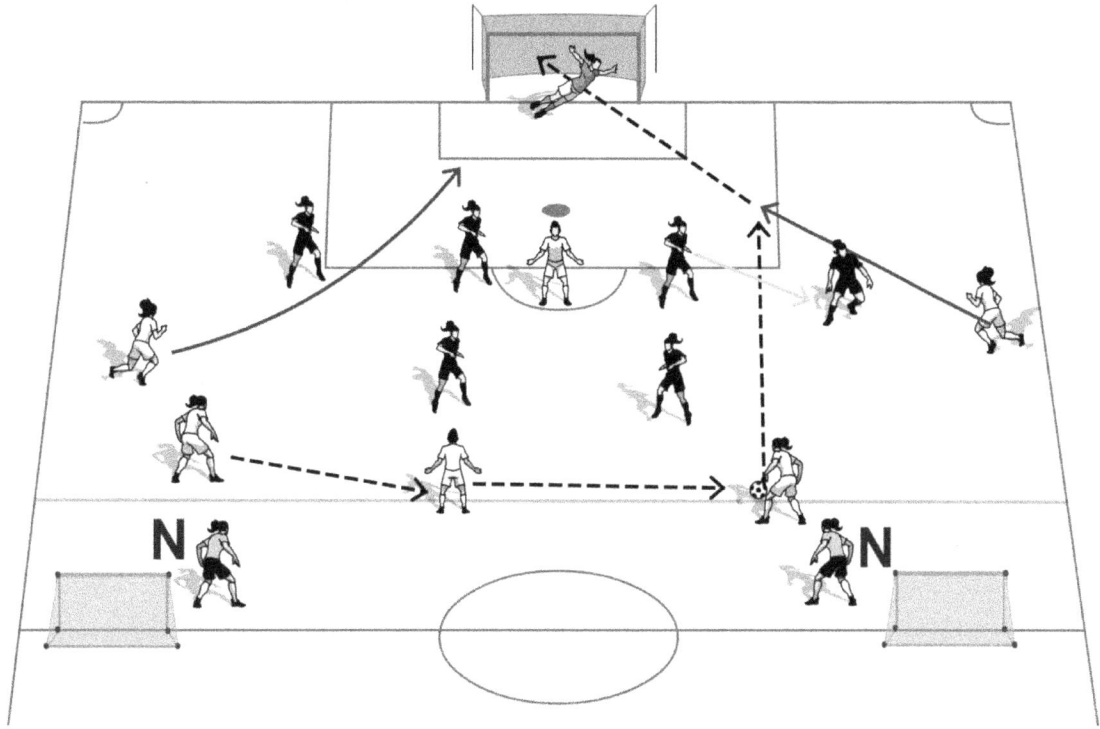

Conditions

- Play begins with the neutral players looking to build up the attack with the possession team.
- The neutral players remain in the middle third as the possession team looks to create a goalscoring opportunity.
- When the defending team wins the ball, they look to score in one of the two smaller goals using the neutral players.

Progressions

- Force the defending side to start higher to restrict their initial space to build up.
- The defending team must score in the middle zone; this will encourage a more aggressive press on transition.

Coaching Points

- Can we use the neutral players to invite a low block out of its shape?
- Can we then move into the newly created space?
- Commit players into the penalty area.
- Change the angle of attack.

7. Creating And Exploiting Overloads

Conditions

- Play starts with the coach, who feeds the ball to the full-back.
- The centre midfielder, winger, and full-back combine to complete at least two passes before releasing the winger into the final third.
- The winger crosses into the penalty area, aiming for the two forward-attacking players.
- If the defenders win the ball, they look to clear the ball into safe areas/mini goals.
- When the move ends, the play restarts from the other side.

Progression

- One attacker and defender from the opposite side join the attack at the far post.

Coaching Points

- In the rondo, look to draw the press away from the winger on the outside.
- Encourage open body shapes and positive first touches for the winger to push the ball into the final third.
- Forwards to create separation from defenders with evasive runs, and to act as targets for the winger crossing the ball.
- Out of Possession – can we block the cross?

8. Overloads in Wide Areas

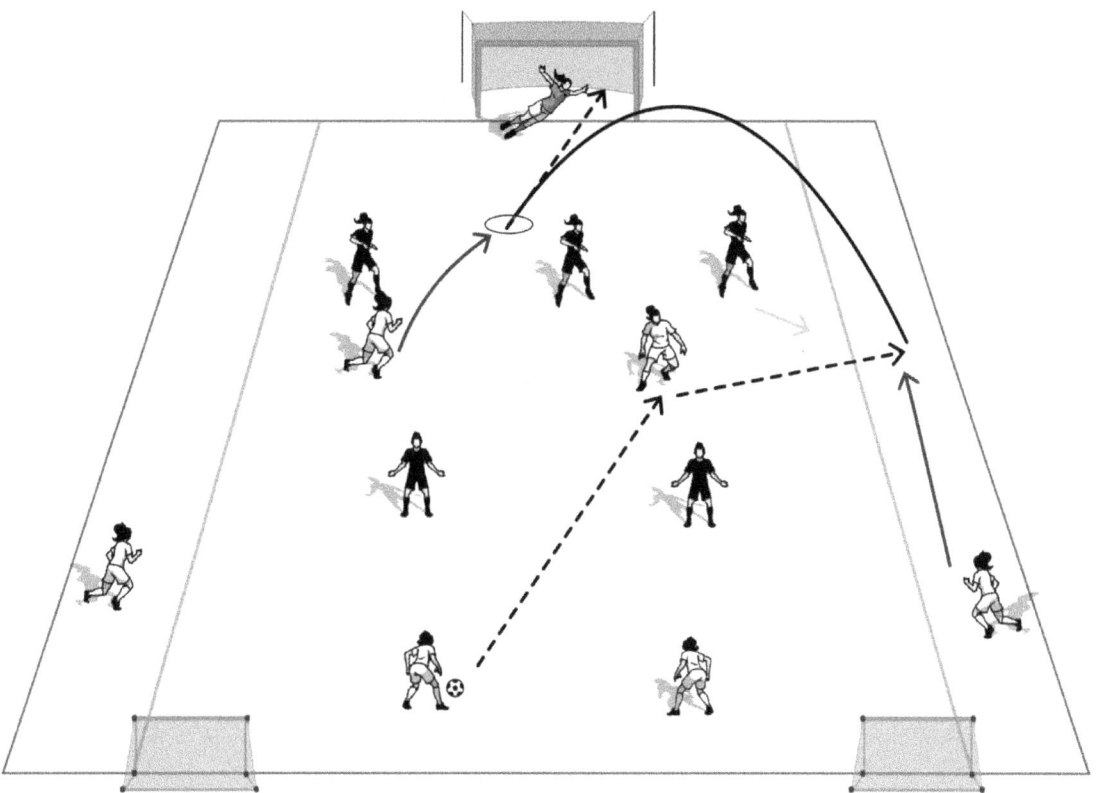

Conditions

- The attacking team start in possession with two centre midfielders, two full-backs, and a two attackers.
- The full-backs are unopposed and are limited to two touches.
- The aim is to create overloads with forward runs to infiltrate the final third.
- The defending team attempts to score in the mini goals when they regain possession.

Progression

- Make the full-backs opposed.

Coaching Points

- Move the ball quickly to attack available space.
- Break lines with vertical passes.
- Identify and exploit the overload.
- When the defence is set, can we change the point of attack?
- Out of Possession – can we protect the area in front of goal?

9. Creating Overloads In The Final Third

Conditions

- The attacking team starts in possession on the halfway line.
- The wide areas are cornered off, and one defender can enter only after the ball has entered.
- A maximum of two attackers are allowed to enter the corner zone.
- When the defending team win the ball, they look to score in the mini goals.

Progressions

- Make it 3v2 in wide areas.
- Remove the zones completely.

Coaching Points

- Maximise the space whilst in possession.
- Can we isolate the full-back with the wingers' positioning?
- Can we break a line to get behind the defensive line?
- Can we fill the penalty area and create targets for the winger's cross.
- Out of Possession – can we make recovery runs and remain compact?

10. Defending Attacks From Wide Areas

Conditions

- The attacking team starts in possession and looks to play passes into wide areas.
- The attacking team follows passes and looks to occupy the penalty area.
- The defending team cannot drop into the penalty area until the pass wide has been made.
- When the defending team regains possession, they look to counter-attack.

Progression

- Increase/decrease the number of players allowed in the penalty area.

Coaching Points

- Defend the goal.
- Protect the central areas.
- Try to remain compact.
- Look to block the pass centrally.
- Recover quickly to defend the cross.
- In possession – can we force the defending team to face its own goal?

11. Defending The Overload

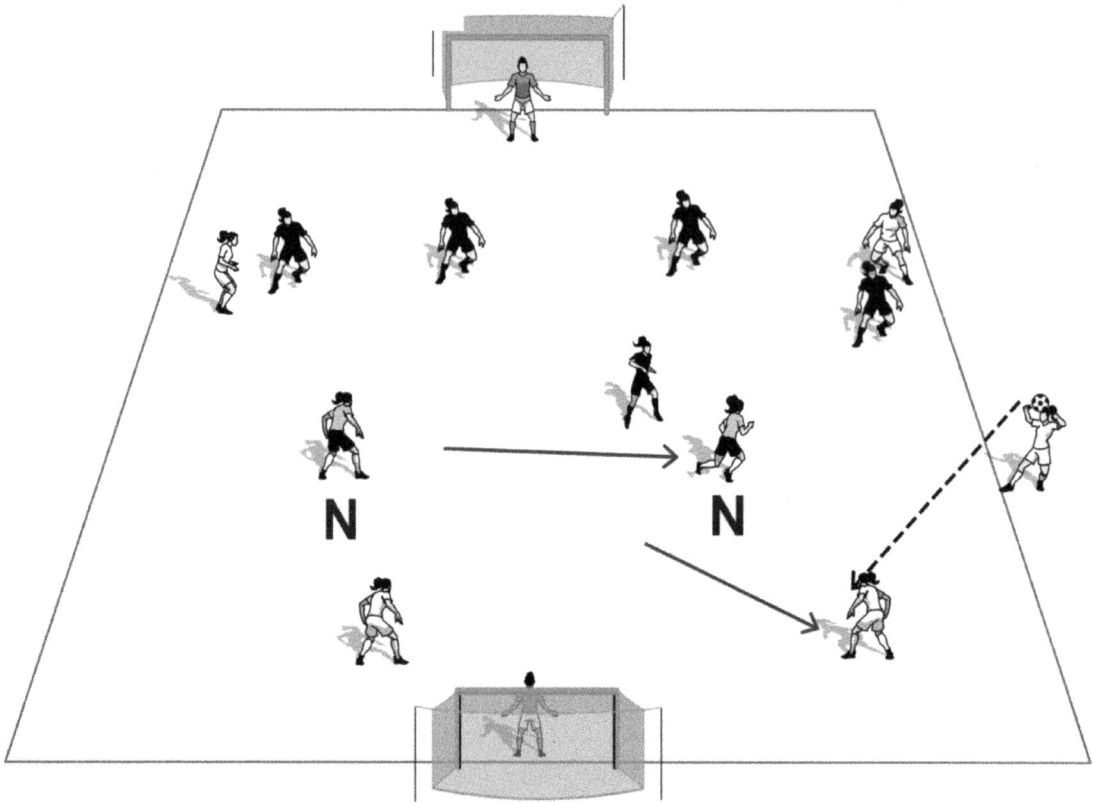

Conditions

- The possession team look to score a goal using the two neutral players.
- The defending team looks to remain compact and delay the attack.
- When the ball goes out of play, it will restart with a throw-in.

Progressions

- Remove neutral players.
- Increase the space.

Coaching Points

- Pressure on the player nearest the ball.
- Defending team must communicate to pass players on.
- Leave the furthest player.
- Force the opponent away from goal.
- Force the opponent backwards.

12. Wave Practice

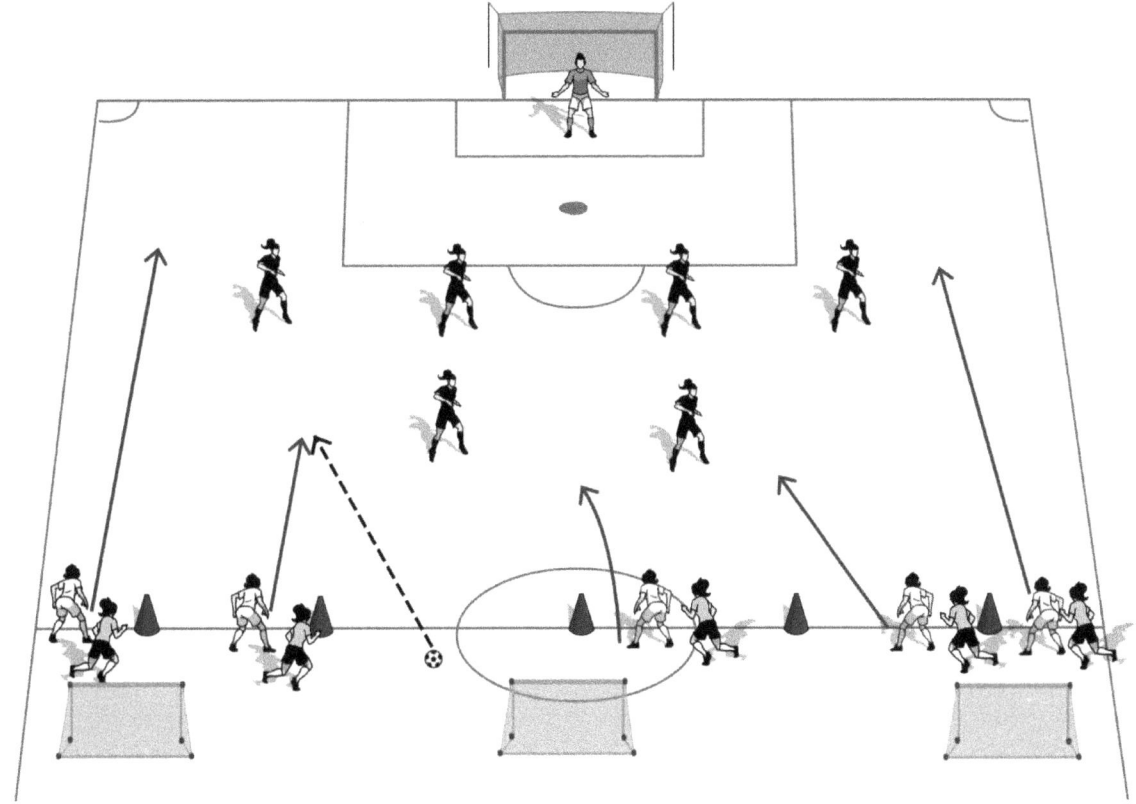

Conditions

- Play begins with the coach playing a ball into the attacking team.
- The attacking team looks to break down the defence's low block to score a goal.
- When the attacking team's possession ends (the first wave), the next team begin their attack (the second wave).
- If the defending team wins back possession, they look to play a pass into one of the mini goals.

Progression

- Instead of playing into the mini goals, the defending team plays into the waiting wave to speed the transition from attack to defence.

Coaching Points

- Can we move the ball quickly to penetrate the opponent's back line?
- Encourage creativity in the final third.
- Can we be patient with the final pass?
- Can we change the angle of attack if the low block is well-positioned defensively?

13. General Practices

The aim of this chapter is to provide you with a number of arrival activities, general practices and activation exercises (delete as applicable) that complement the main practices found in Chapters 6, 9 and 12. These practices focus less on pitch geography and more on reinforcing your playing principles with a greater focus on the technical side.

Key

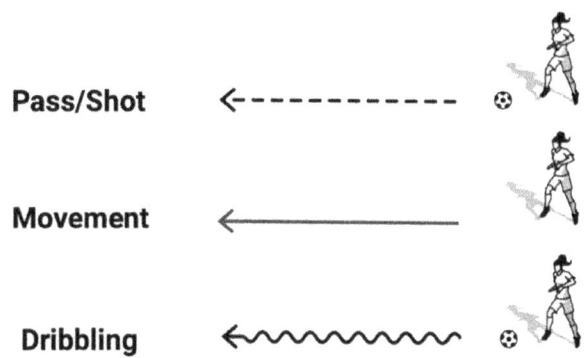

Reminders

- Throughout these practices, where I have included goalkeepers, this is to demonstrate how they can be used in the practice. If there are no goalkeepers, then they can be substituted for a mini goal or gate with a condition such as a 'two touch finish'.
- I have used the same number of players throughout the practices for uniformity, but have designed them so they can be adjusted for 8-18 players. If you are working with an odd number of players, working with a neutral player or 'magic player' should not impact the realism of the practice too greatly.
- Where I have used multiple goals or poles, this is to demonstrate the target that players are aiming to play to or through. Where mini goals or poles are unavailable, I would use cones in their place.
- Pitch size and timings have been deliberately left off; this is because you will know what works best for your players.

1. Double Rondo Box: Playing Away From Pressure

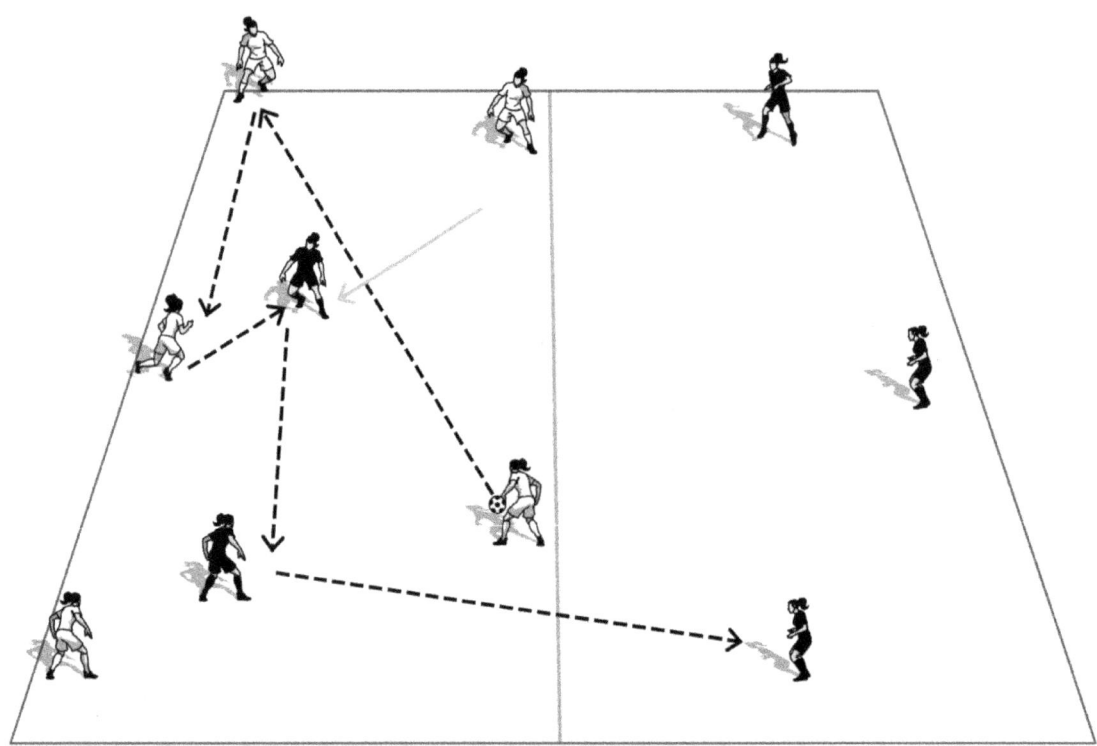

Conditions

- The teams are divided into two zones.
- When the ball is played into one zone, that team will look to retain possession, whilst two players from the opposite zone will look to regain the ball.
- When the defending players regain possession, they look to play back into the other half.

Progressions

- An extra defender can transition across to increase the press.
- Continue to add pressing players to increase the challenge for the possession team.

Coaching Points

- Make the space as big as possible for the team in possession.
- Think about body shapes to receive the ball.
- Break a line to beat the press.
- Movement off-the-ball.
- Out of Possession – make the space as compact as possible as quickly as possible.

2. Switch play – Four-Corner Game

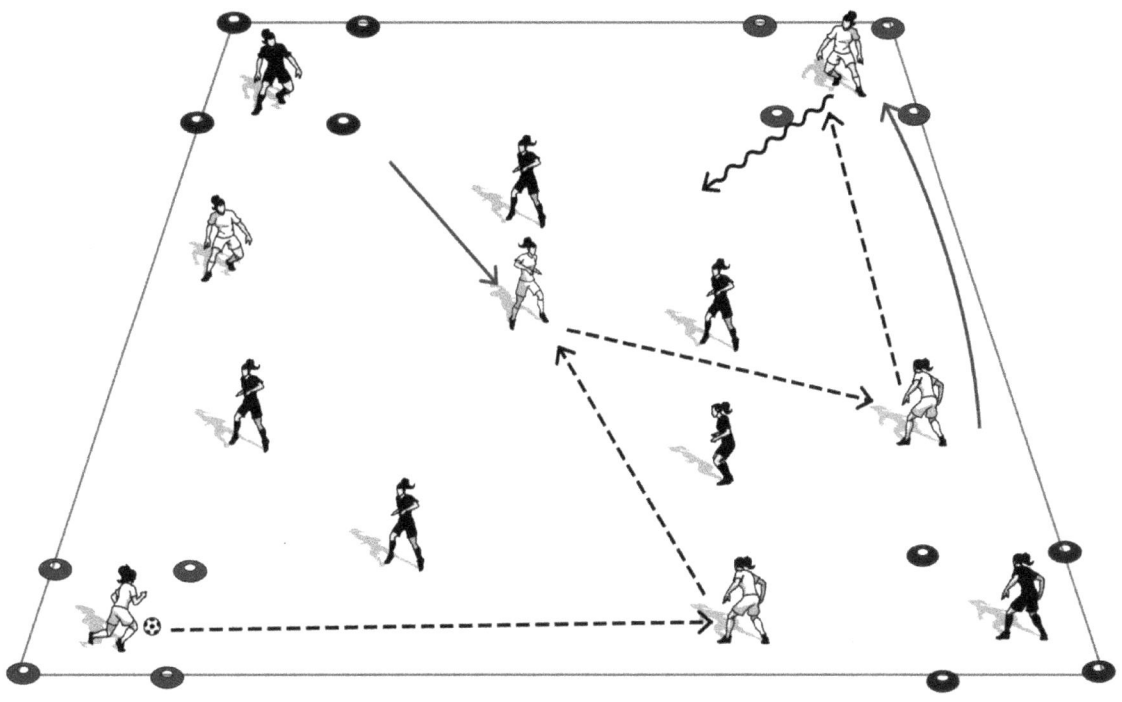

Conditions

- The team in possession looks to switch play from one corner to the other.
- When the player in the corner receives the pass, they step out of the box and are replaced by the player they receive the pass from.

Progressions

- Add a halfway line to restrict space and increase the intensity of the press.
- Increase the number of passes allowed before players can rotate.

Coaching Points

- Encourage off-the-ball rotation.
- Break a line.
- Out of Possession – Close the space to the ball as quickly as possible.
- Out of Possession – Remain compact in central areas.

3. Goalkeeper Transition Rondo

Conditions

- Play starts with the goalkeeper, who plays to the team on the outside of the zone. They look to retain possession.
- The possession team looks to complete five passes before scoring in a mini goal.
- When the defending team wins the ball, they look to combine to score past the goalkeeper.

Progression

- When the possession team loses the ball, allow one defender to come inside and protect the goal.
- Increase/decrease the number of passes before the possession team scores.

Coaching Points

- Correct body shape to receive the ball.
- Understand where we're aiming to send the ball *before* doing so.
- Balance to receive and release the pass in one fluent motion.
- Goalkeeper to recover from their in possession to out of possession stance.
- Out of Possession – Forwards to combine to create goalscoring opportunities.

4. Creating Overloads – Finishing In The Final Third

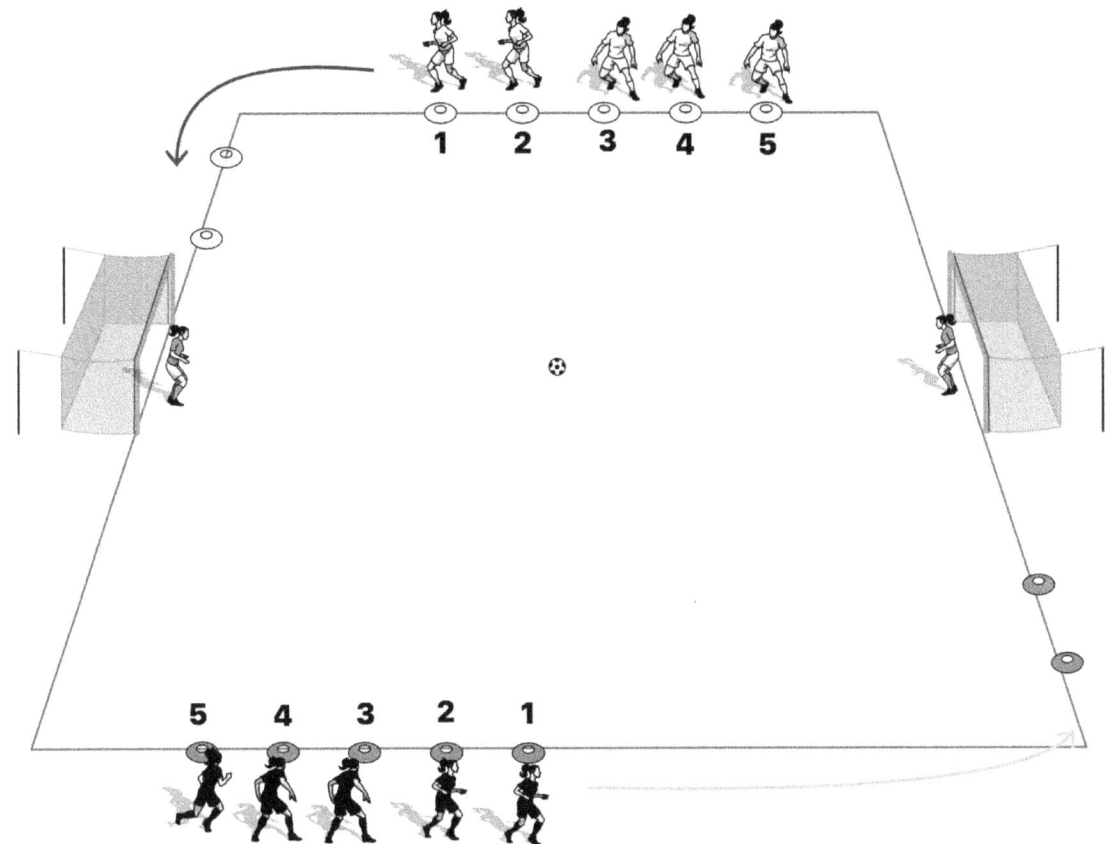

Conditions

- Players line up on the sideline and are numbered.
- The coach calls out a number; this is the trigger for the practice to begin.
- Players whose number gets called run around to the gate next to the goal they are defending, before entering the field of play.
- If 1v1, the player with the ball must complete a take-on before scoring.
- If 2v2, the players in possession must complete at least one pass before scoring.

Progressions

- Increase the number of players in the game gradually.
- Delay the call of numbers so people join later; force the team to wait until they are on the field before they can score.

Coaching Points

- Encourage creativity.
- Encourage taking on defenders.
- Movement off-the-ball.
- Out of Possession – Force away from goal.

5. Four-Corner High Pressing Intensity

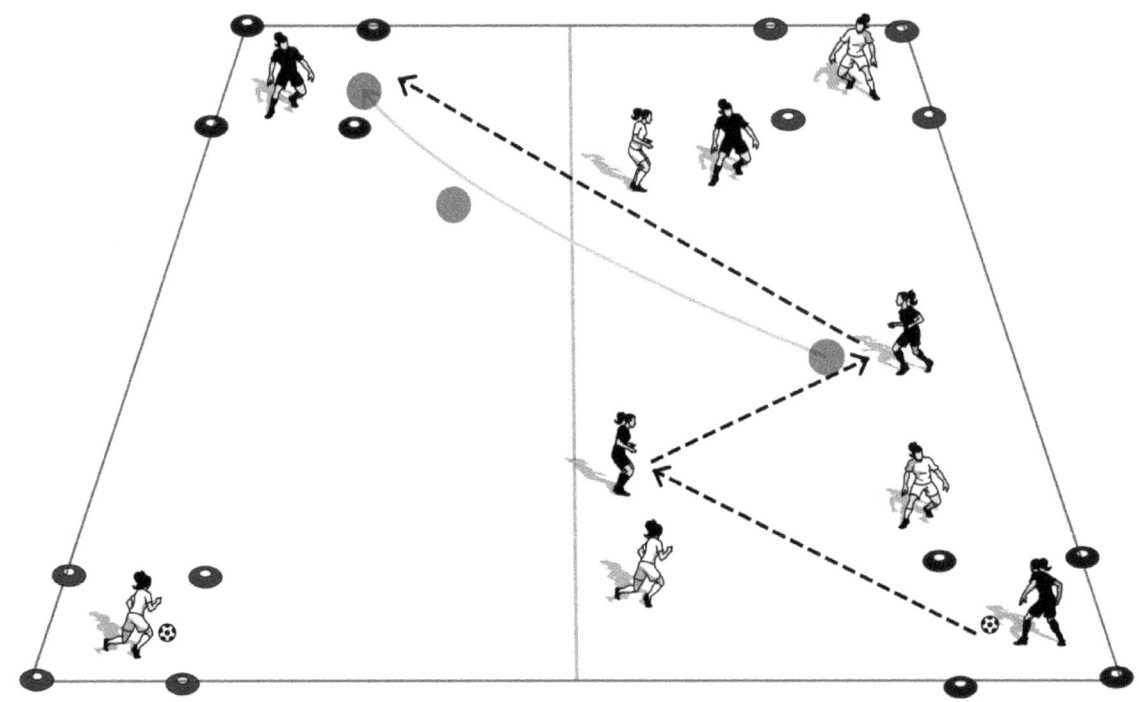

Conditions

- Everyone except the four corner players starts in one half.
- The team in possession must complete three passes before switching the play.
- Everyone must move across to the opposite half with the switch.
- Players on the outside rotate when they receive the ball.

Progression

- Increase the number of passes.
- Remove the halfway line.

Coaching Points

- Focus on the correct body shape and balance to receive the ball.
- Think about off-the-ball movement.
- Can we create space away from the ball?

6. Three-Team Pressing Zone

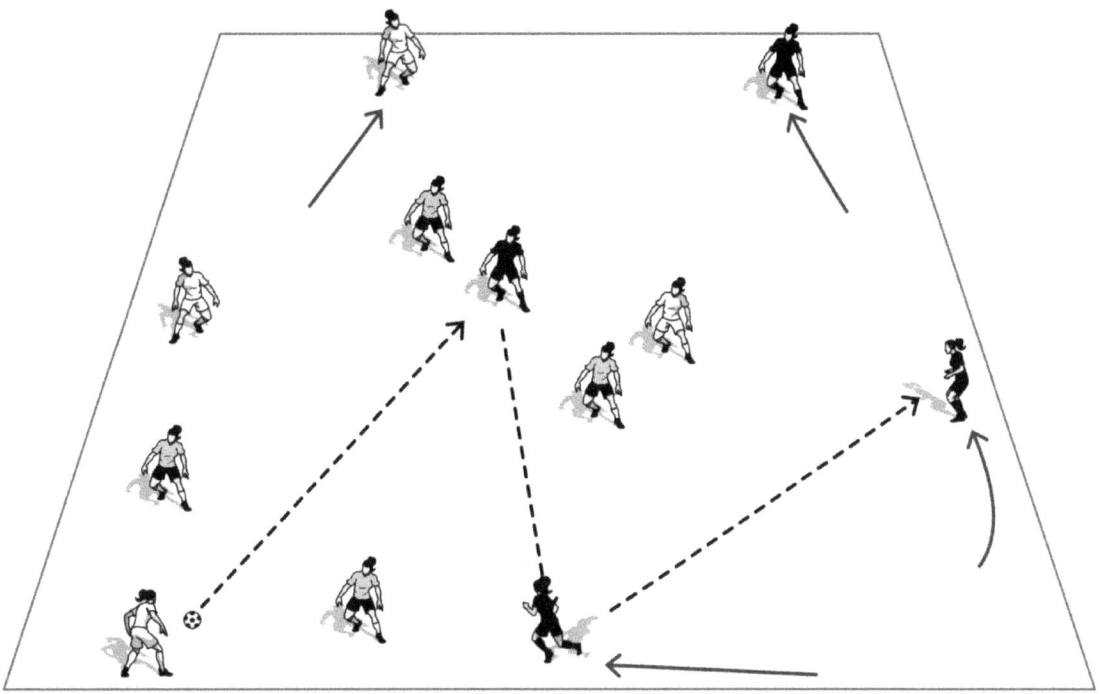

Conditions

- Two teams start in possession of the ball. The third team looks to press the ball.
- When the team in possession loses possession, they replace the third team as the pressing team.
- Play continues with the two teams in possession.

Progression

- Change the shape/size of the space used. Hexagon/Octagon/Circle.
- Limit Touches.

Regression

- Make the space bigger to increase the room to pass.
- Make the space smaller to decrease the physical demands of the press.

Coaching Points

- Make as much of the pitch as visible as possible.
- Utilise positional spacing to force the defending team to cover a big area.
- Multiple options around the ball.
- Movement away from the ball.

7. Double-Box Rondo

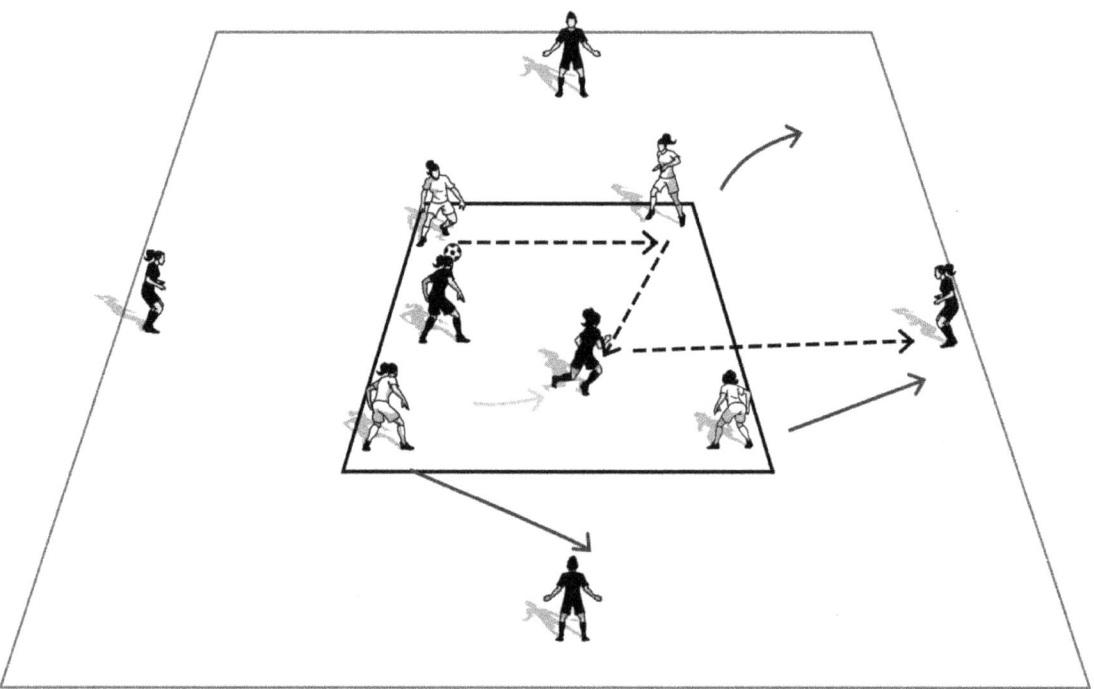

Conditions

- Play begins inside the smaller box with a rondo.
- The possession team must keep the ball against the press of the defence.
- When the defending team knocks the ball out of the zone, the bigger zone comes into play. The possession team transition to out of possession and look to win the ball back.

Progression

- Add an additional defender into the middle zone.
- Rotate the central players.

Coaching Points

- Make the space as big as possible for whichever team is in possession.
- Rotate positions in the space created.
- Open body shapes to receive the ball.
- Communication.
- Out of Possession – remain compact.

8. Defending The Line

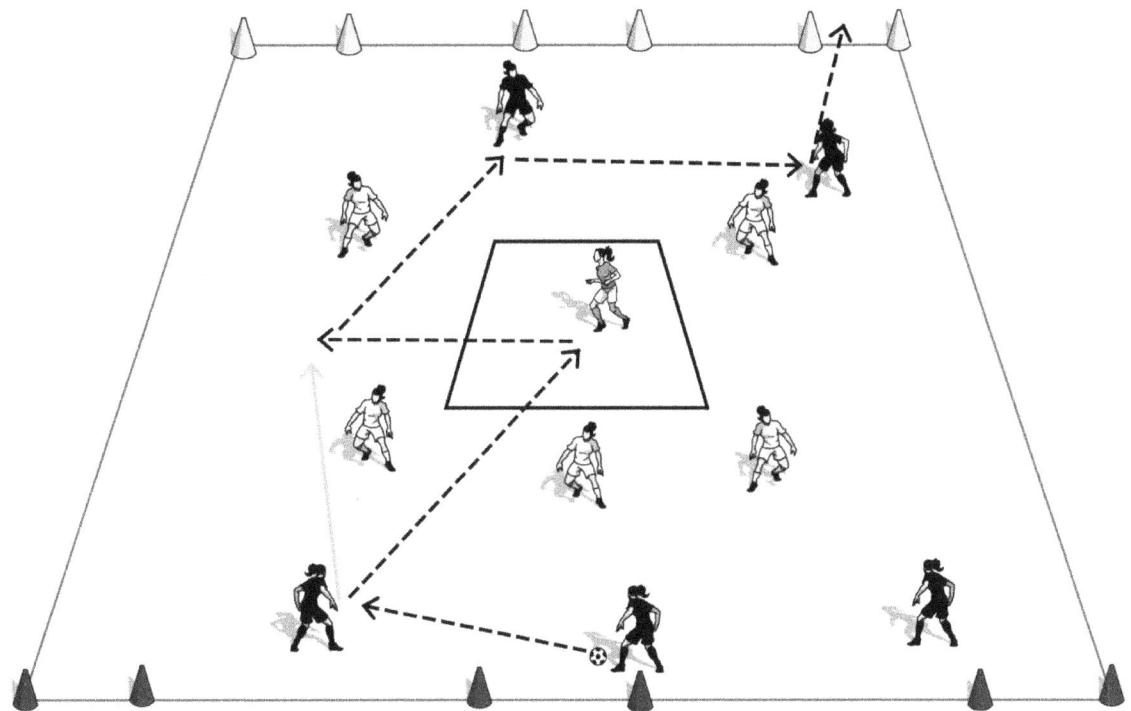

Conditions

- The possession team start and commence play through the goalkeeper/neutral player before looking to score in one of the small goals.
- The neutral/goalkeeper is unopposed.
- The defending team looks to remain compact and defend the central areas.
- When the opponent wins back the ball, they look to score as quickly as possible in any goal.

Progression

- Allow the neutral player to leave the central zone and have players rotate in to receive the ball.
- Remove the central zone and make the goalkeeper/neutral player opposed.

Coaching Points

- Prevent the possession team from breaking lines centrally.
- Defend the space centrally.
- Remain compact and narrow to force the opponent into wide areas.
- Close the distance to the ball.

9. Three Team, Three Zone, Beating The Press

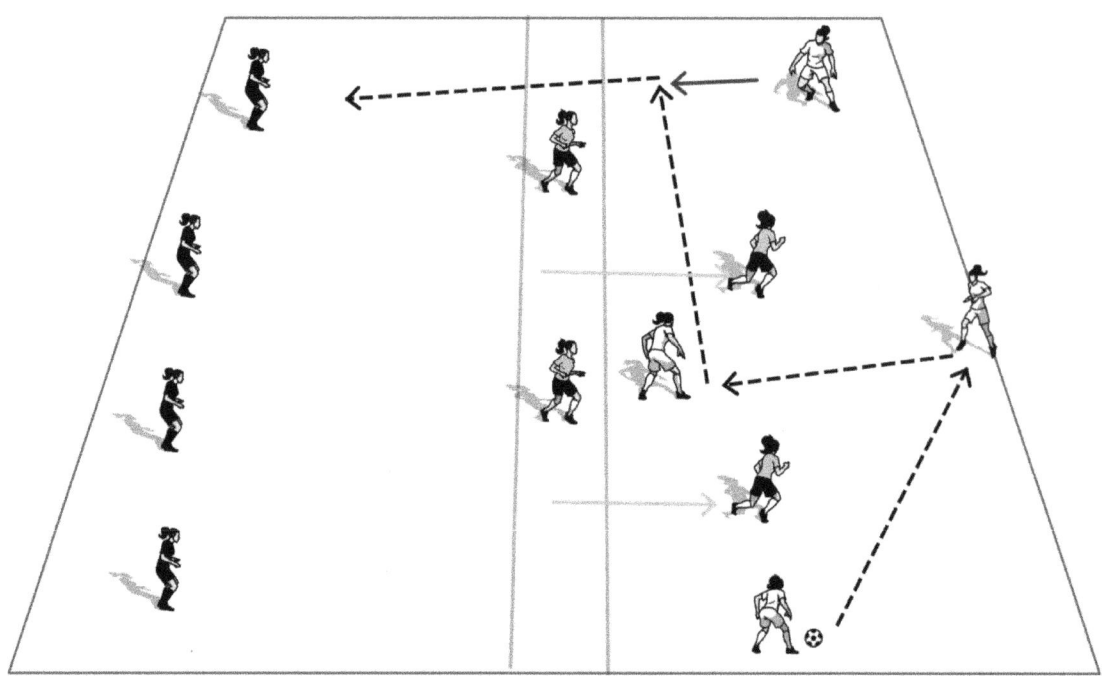

Conditions

- Three teams all start in their own zone.
- The coach plays a ball into one end, triggering two players from the neutral zone to press.
- The possession team must complete five passes before switching play to the opposite zone.
- If the possession team switches successfully, the remaining middle zone players press.
- If the team wins possession, they swap places and the team losing possession becomes the pressing team.

Progressions

- Increase/decrease the number of passes before the switch.
- Increase the number of players who can press.

Coaching Points

- Make the space as big as possible to create space.
- Rotate into the space to create passing options.
- Ready players' body shapes to receive the ball to switch play.
- Out of Possession – defend the line.
- Out of Possession – block through passes.

10. Creating Overloads In The Final Third Finishing

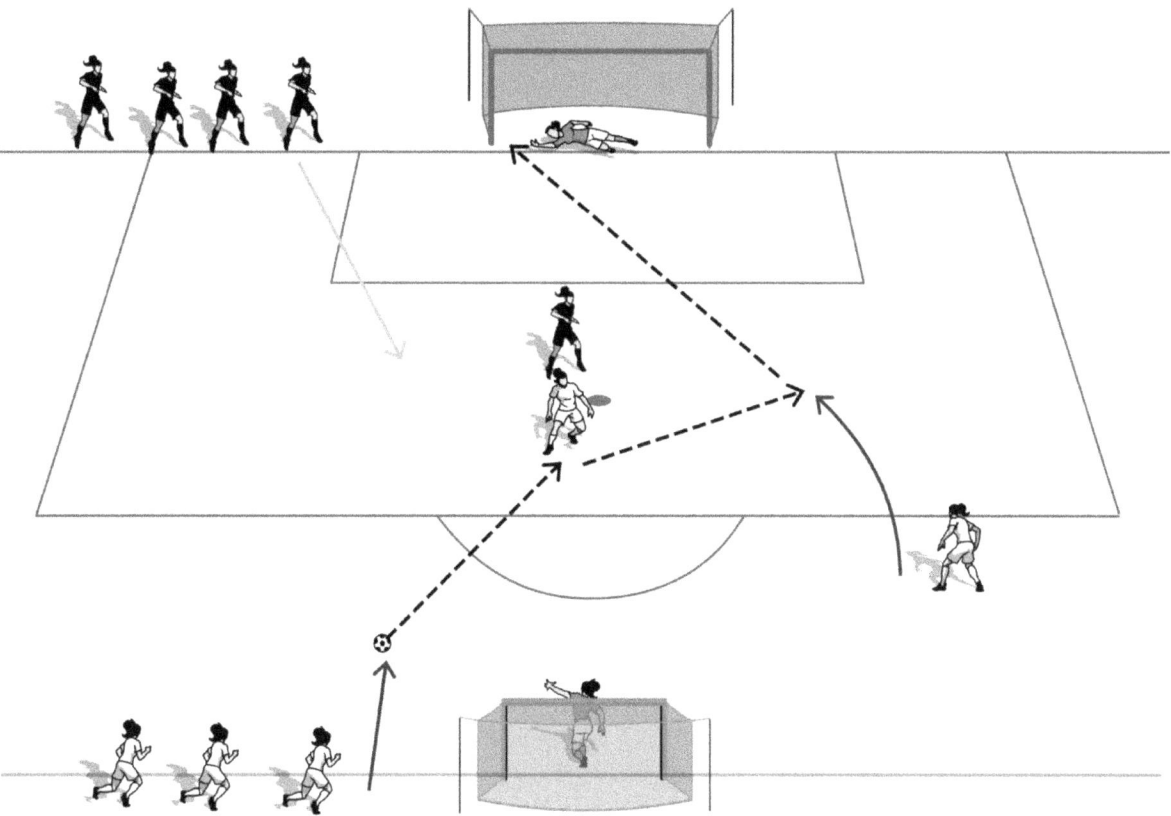

Conditions

- The practice begins with the attacking team, which starts in a 1v1.
- When the player has scored or missed, two players from the opposite team join the attack and the first player transitions to defend the goal.
- The two teams alternate the overload until everyone is involved.

Progressions

- Introduce a shot clock to speed up the attack.

Coaching Points

- Direct passes to break lines.
- Early shots to disrupt the defence.
- Finding the free player.
- Out of Possession – show the attacking team away from goal.
- Out of Possession – close down the nearest player.

11. Changing The Point Of Attack

Conditions

- The team starting in possession looks to attack the goals end to end.
- After a goal is scored, the direction of attack is changed to attack the side goals.
- When another goal is scored, the focus of the attack switches back to the end goals.

Progressions

- Retain possession of the ball when a goal is scored.
- Change the direction of play every time the ball goes dead.

Coaching Points

- Quick movement/rotation to change the angle of attack.
- Make the space as big as possible when in possession.
- Break lines to score.
- Out of Possession – protect the nearest goal.
- Out of Possession – drop to protect the space.
- Out of Possession – make the opposition's play predictable.
- Out of Possession – delay the attack.

12. Six-Goal Game

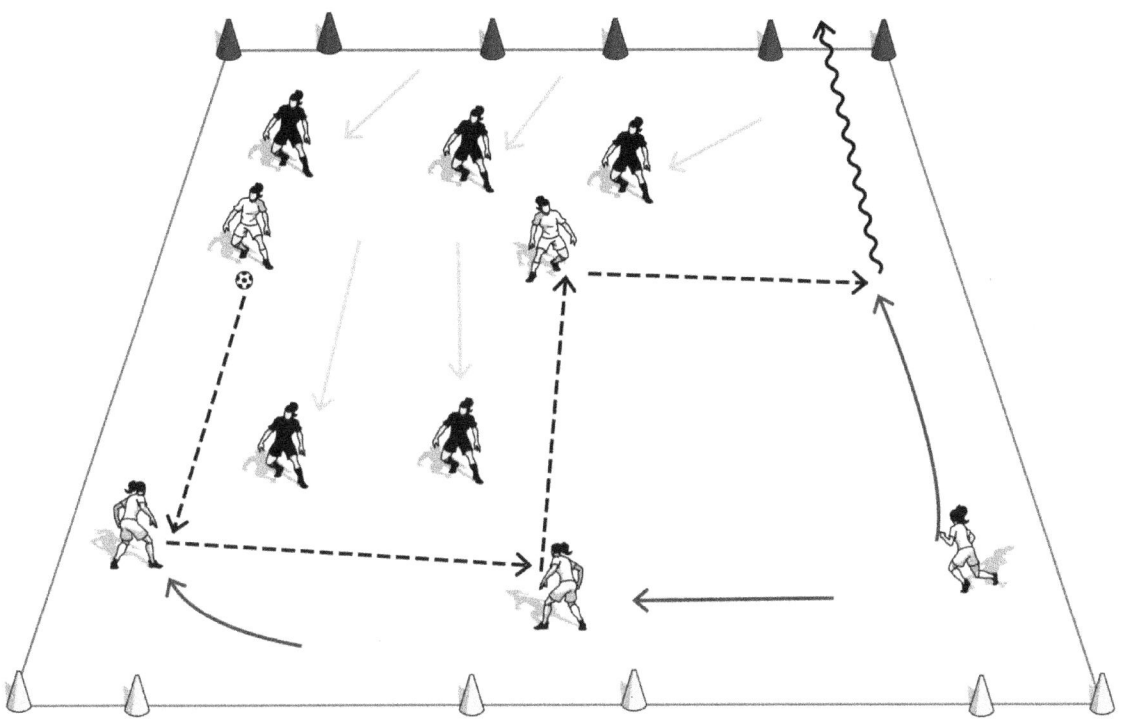

Conditions

- Game 1: Teams attempt to score in the outside goals only.
- Game 2: Teams attempt to score in all three goals.
- Game 3: Once a goal has been scored in, the scoring team cannot score in the same goal.
- Game 4: First to three. Players are handed a bib each and must rotate to drop their bib in goal after scoring.

Coaching Points

- Quick movement/rotation to change the angle of attack.
- Make the space as big as possible when in possession.
- Break lines to score.
- Out of Possession – defend the space nearest goal.
- Remain compact and narrow.
- Delay the opponent to force them backwards.

14. Conclusion

Make It Work For You!

I have always tried to pass on help and information to coaches looking to progress, in the same way that other coaches helped me when I began coaching. I've always tried to maintain an open-door policy on training sessions for any coach wishing to come and observe. One of the first things I always tell them is to *challenge* what they see. I want them not just to look at what I do well, but at what I do not do well! I ask them to think about how they would do things better.

Initially, when writing this book, I thought I could get enough practices down on paper to support coaches. However, I soon realised that this approach failed to capture what I feel is one of the most important considerations for any session: "Is what I am coaching *relevant* for my players?"

Whilst my ego may take a bruising, I acknowledge that not everything you read within these pages will necessarily work for you, your coaching style, or your team. However, if you've read through the previous 13 chapters and thought, "Rubbish, I'd do it this way", then – weirdly – I consider that a success! As strange as it sounds, much of what I wanted from this book was to provide the foundation for a coach to build from. In turn, I also wanted something from which they would ask questions. If you're reading through this book and thinking about how you would adapt a session, or how you would make a different coaching point, then for me, that's most of the battle.

The Planning

When I first started coaching, I would consume so many coaching books, trying to fill the gaps in my knowledge; I would often be disappointed if I purchased a book that didn't provide me with all the answers. What I didn't understand was that it wasn't just what the book was saying, it was also what it *wasn't* saying. I still needed to think for myself and adapt what I was reading to suit the needs of my players.

Before each practice, I spent so much time planning my session to make it 'perfect', ensuring every detail was correct and every player had a purpose. I'd visualise in my mind how I saw the session would go, what I'd say, and how I would say it. However, I failed to plan for contingencies in things that I could not control. This meant that I was a very inflexible coach.

The experience of writing this book has forced me to think about the things that I cannot control in a session, encouraging me to think on my feet and adapt my sessions (often on the spot). One night, these skills were really put to the test as I turned up to a session with no bibs, cones, or balls! It wasn't quite the scene from

Mike Bassett: England Manager, where the training balls are locked in Lonnie's car, but it wasn't far off.

The Execution

To quote the top author of several excellent coaching books, Gary Curneen, "There's no substitute for getting out on the grass." Since I began writing, I have been very fortunate to deliver a number of sessions from within these pages to different teams, with the focus being on how they can be adapted to different audiences. In each instance, although sessions might have looked the same on paper, they looked very different when tailored to the players being coached!

When we're on the grass – synthetic or real – it's really critical that we focus on what is in front of us and coach accordingly. If something isn't right in a session, then we need to make sure we adjust correspondingly. You may be forced to problem-solve to get the outcomes you require.

On one of my UEFA B licence assessments, we were asked to create overloads. My partner and I designed what we felt was a simple session to create overloads in the final third. The only problem turned out to be a big one... the players couldn't get it into the final third! Suddenly, my session was all about fixing *this* issue so that my partner could coach the session we'd originally designed. On this occasion, I might have been forgiven for just trying to focus on my coaching points, but it was important to recognise what was happening in front of me and modify things accordingly.

The Reflection

Football is an ever-evolving sport, with new tactics and strategies emerging regularly. Reflective coaches are more open to change and innovation, as they constantly seek ways to improve their coaching methods based on what they have learned from past experiences.

You are going to do good things. Yet, no team or coach is perfect, and mistakes will happen. Once you've planned, adjusted and delivered, it's time to reflect on what you've done. We have all come away from a session thinking, "If only I'd done that", as we're pulling out of the car park.

Coaching can be a highly emotional role, especially during high-pressure situations like crucial matches. Reflection helps the coach gain perspective and manage their emotions effectively. A great session can have you bouncing for days; likewise, a terrible session can make you question everything.

Reflecting on both successes and failures provides valuable insights into what went wrong and why. Reflection is crucial to aid you as a coach; learning from mistakes enables us to avoid repeating them. By reviewing our emotional responses to different situations, we can maintain composure and make better decisions under pressure. We reflect not to rationalise – nor to accept or defer blame – but to focus on improvement for the future.

Do It Your Way!

Coaching is a continuous cycle of learning and improvement. You will have moments when you think you've taken a step forward, and you'll have moments when you feel like giving up and walking away. The skill is not only trying to make the good moments outnumber the bad moments, but being able to deal with the bad ones when they come your way. Coaching is a role that requires passion and dedication; when you are true to yourself, you are more likely to find fulfilment and stay motivated in your coaching journey over the long term.

Be authentic to who you are and do things your way. Coaching is about building genuine relationships. When you are yourself, you show authenticity, and people can relate to you more easily. Players appreciate coaches who are real and sincere, and an environment of trust and openness is created.

While being authentic is crucial, being yourself also means being open to growth and learning. Authentic coaches are more willing to adapt their methods to suit the ever-changing needs of their environments.

Being yourself when coaching is not only important for your personal well-being and satisfaction, but also for fostering meaningful connections with your players and creating a supportive and successful team environment. Embracing authenticity allows you to lead with integrity and inspire your players to be the best versions of themselves. It starts by trying to be the best version of yourself!

Now, get out there and get on the grass!

Some of our other 30+ football coaching books

BennionKearny.com/soccer

www.ingramcontent.com/pod-product-compliance
Lightning Source LLC
Chambersburg PA
CBHW061057170426
43194CB00025B/2961